Jewelry
for the
New Romantic

Unexpected Techniques with Crystals and Beading Wire

Nealay Patel

Kalmbach Books
21027 Crossroads Circle
Waukesha, Wisconsin 53186
www.Kalmbach.com/Books

Illustrations by the author. Photography by Kalmbach Books.

Published in 2011
15 14 13 12 11   1 2 3 4 5

Manufactured in the United States of America

ISBN: 978-0-87116-427-8

Edited by Erica Swanson
Art Direction by Lisa Bergman
Layout by Lisa Schroeder

Publisher's Cataloging-In-Publication Data

Patel, Nealay.

  Jewelry for the new romantic : unexpected techniques with crystals and beading wire / Nealay Patel.

    p. : ill. (some col.) ; cm.

  ISBN: 978-0-87116-427-8

  1. Beadwork--Patterns. 2. Beadwork--Handbooks, manuals, etc. 3. Jewelry making--Handbooks, manuals, etc. I. Title. II. Title: New romantic

TT860 .P28 2011

745.594/2

Contents

Acknowledgments

A special thanks to all who have purchased this book and support the author and designer. You are the reason why I continue to share my knowledge, exploration, and passion with the world.

I would like to thank everyone involved with the making of this book. To Dane Dudley, Debbie Bryan, Alicia Benton, Theo Arguna, Vanessa Wells, and anyone else involved with this project or inspiring me. Very special thanks to Loretta Nelson, Pat Boudreaux, and Alouette: A Unique Bead Shoppe for providing all my materials for the collection. Thanks to Erica Swanson, Mark Thompson, and everyone at Kalmbach Books for working hard to make this project possible. All of you are awesome and amazing to work with.

Last but not least, a very big thank you to my loving family for their support and encouragement.

Supplies
All of the supplies in this book were provided by Alouettes bead store.

Alouette: A Unique Bead Shoppe
2150 S. Douglas Blvd.
Oklahoma City, OK 73130
405-733-5300
www.alouettebeadsok.com
Alouette40@cox.net

Introduction

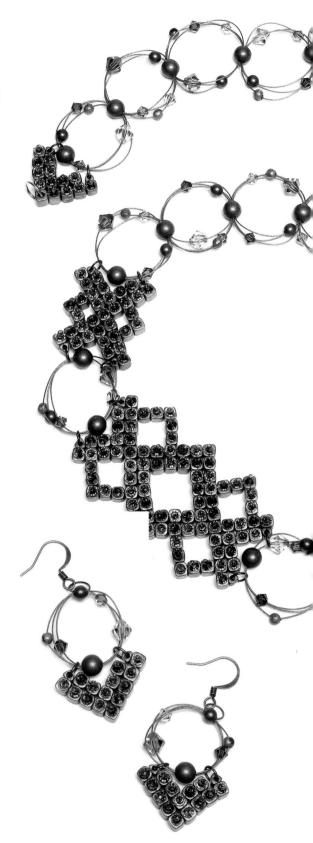

Who would have known beading wire would have so many uses other than just to string beads? I sure didn't until I began to play with it and discover how much fun it was to incorporate it into my stitched beadwork. I showed my ideas to a friend, who then encouraged the idea of creating a jewelry collection that featured beading wire as the central concept. Thus, this book was born.

One of the features of beading wire is how flexible and versatile it is to use. The designs use beading wire as a substitute for metal wire, which unlike beading wire is not very forgiving. Metal wire can kink, break, wear out, tarnish, or scratch with improper handling of the pliers (I speak from experience). I couldn't tell you how many times I messed up a simple project because I bent the wire too much or accidentally scratched it.

After you learn the basic techniques, you'll find that beading wire is durable and easy to use. Because it is easy to work with, these patterns are fun to make. You'll find helpful information about materials and techniques beginning on page 68, or you can find your needle and thread, flip to your favorite project, and start stitching.

Aside from the practicality of using beading wire as the central element of the each design, the artistic direction of the collection came from my take on Edwardian jewelry design. Edwardian jewelry has a very airy and lacy look, and I used beading wire as inspiration to incorporate that aspect into each design.

Each design features new and innovative techniques that are fun and easy to learn, and the designs are also colorful and effortless to wear for any occasion. I really enjoyed putting together this collection of work and writing this book, and I hope you will enjoy reading and using the patterns to re-create the designs.

The Collection

Lose Control

Sometimes, playing with a medium results in a whole new vision for design. This set came about from the first series of sketches I did after I began to work with beading wire. I love the simplicity of the necklace rope and beaded beads, and the crazy swirls of beading wire really livens up the design.

Skill level: Beginner/intermediate

Materials
Necklace, 32 in. (81 cm)
- 7 g 11º seed beads, teal luster
- 7 g 11º cylinder beads, transparent blue gray rainbow luster
- **41** 4 mm bicone crystals, blue zircon
- **16** 4 mm bicone crystals, indicolite
- **56** 3 mm bicone crystals, indicolite
- **8** 10 mm helix crystals, crystal
- **7** 16 mm round glass pearls, light gray
- **15** 3 mm round glass pearls, light gray
- toggle clasp
- **11** 2 mm crimp tubes
- **11** 4 mm crimp covers
- 2 yd. (1.8 m) beading wire, .019, sterling silver
- 1 yd. (.9 m) beading wire, .014
- tool kit, p. 71

Note: All findings are sterling silver.

Techniques
Starting new thread, p. 74
Attaching new thread, p. 74
Securing thread, p. 75
Folded crimp, p. 75
Flattened crimp, p. 76
Applying a crimp cover, p. 76

Necklace

Beaded Beads

1 Cut a comfortable length of beading thread and pick up four 11º seed beads, a 3 mm indicolite bicone, four cylinder beads, a 4 mm blue zircon crystal bicone, four cylinder beads, a 3 mm crystal bicone, and three seed beads. Go back through the first seed bead to form a loop.

2 Pick up five seed beads, a 3 mm bicone, four cylinder beads, a 4 mm blue zircon bicone, and four cylinder beads. Go up through the first 3 mm bicone added in the previous stitch, and the seed bead above it from the previous loop. Pick up two seed beads and go through the second seed bead of the five previously strung (**figure 1**). Repeat this stitch again to create a third loop.

figure 1

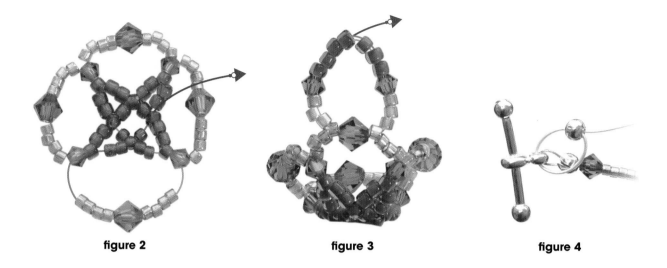

figure 2   figure 3   figure 4

3 Pick up four seed beads and go down through the first of the three seed beads added in step 1 and the 3 mm bicone of the very first loop. Pick up four cylinders, a 4 mm blue zircon bicone, and four cylinders, and go up through the 3 mm bicone and the seed bead above it in the third loop. Pick up two seed beads and go through the second seed bead of the four that were previously strung. Pick up a seed bead and go through the first seed bead added in step 1 to complete the bead cap (**figure 2**).

4 Go through the seed beads until the thread exits left of a 4 mm blue zircon bicone and the following cylinder bead.

5 Pick up three cylinder beads, a 3 mm bicone, seven seed beads, a 3 mm bicone, and three cylinder beads, and go through the cylinder bead to the right of the 4 mm bicone, and the 4 mm blue zircon bicone and the next cylinder of the current loop (**figure 3**).

6 Go through the beads until the thread exits the fourth seed bead (or the top) of the new loop. Repeat step 2 to create the second and third loop, except go though the cylinders on both sides of the 4 mm blue zircon bicone. Before stitching the last loop, insert the 16 mm blue zircon glass pearl.

7 Complete the final loop and secure the thread to finish the beaded bead.

8 Create a total of seven beaded beads.

Stringing the Necklace

1 Cut a 40-in. (1.02 m) length of beading wire and place a Bead Stopper on one end.

2 Pick up the following beads: a 4 mm indicolite bicone, 35 cylinder beads, a 10 mm helix crystal, 35 cylinder beads, a 4 mm indicolite bicone, and a beaded bead. Repeat this pattern until all seven beaded beads are strung. End the pattern with the 4 mm indicolite bicone and attach the toggle clasp to the necklace rope by picking up a crimp tube and the toggle clasp. Pass the wire through the crimp tube again and crimp the crimp tube. Apply a crimp cover.

Weaving the Sterling Silver Beading Wire

1 Cut a 2-yd. (1.8 m) length of sterling silver beading wire. Pick up a crimp tube and pass the wire through one of the clasp ends and into the crimp tube to create a small loop. Crimp the crimp tube and apply a crimp cover (**figure 4**).

2 Loosely curl 5–7 in. (13–18 cm) of the wire by gently pulling the wire between your index finger and thumbnail. Pick up seven to ten seed beads, a 3 mm light gray pearl, and a 4 mm blue zircon bicone. Wrap the curled wire around the necklace rope, and continue to curl and bead the next 5–7 in. Between each set or two sets, make a folded crimp on the wire and place a crimp cover over it. This will keep the beads from shifting as the necklace is worn.

3 Secure the end of the sterling silver wire: Pick up one crimp tube, pass the wire around the other clasp end and into the crimp tube, and then crimp it. Apply a crimp cover to finish the necklace design.

Bracelet

1 Create five beaded beads, following steps 1–7 of "Beaded Beads."

2 Cut 12 in. (31 cm) of beading wire and place a Bead Stopper at one end. Pick up the following beads: a 4 mm indicolite bicone, a cylinder, a 10 mm helix crystal, a cylinder, a 4 mm indicolite bicone, and a beaded bead. Repeat this pattern until all five beaded beads are strung. End the pattern with the 4 mm indicolite bicone and attach the toggle clasp to both ends as in step 2 of "Stringing the Necklace."

3 Cut 24 in. (61 cm) of sterling silver beading wire and follow steps 1–3 of "Weaving the Sterling Silver Beading Wire" to complete the bracelet design.

Materials

Bracelet, 8 in. (20 cm)

- 3–4 g 11º seed beads, teal luster
- 3–4 g 11º cylinder beads, transparent blue gray rainbow luster
- **27–30** 4 mm bicone crystals, blue zircon
- **12** 4 mm bicone crystals, indicolite
- **40** 3 mm bicone crystals, indicolite
- **6** 10 mm helix crystals, crystal
- **5** 16 mm round glass pearls, light gray
- **5** 3 mm glass round pearls, light gray
- toggle clasp
- **7** 2 mm crimp tubes
- **7** 4 mm crimp covers
- 24 in. (61 cm) beading wire, .019, sterling silver
- 12 in. (30 cm) beading wire, .014
- tool kit, p. 71

Note: All findings are sterling silver.

Techniques

Starting new thread, p. 74
Attaching a new thread, p. 74
Securing thread, p. 75
Folded crimp, p. 75
Flattened crimp, p. 76
Applying a crimp cover, p. 76

Earrings

1 Create two beaded beads following steps 1–7 from "Beaded Beads."

2 Pick up a 4 mm indicolite bicone, a beaded bead, and a 4 mm indicolite bicone on an eye pin and make a simple loop.

3 Pick up a 3 mm light gray round glass pearl, a 10 mm helix crystal, and 10 cylinder beads on a head pin and make a simple loop.

4 Attach the crystal dangle and an earring hook to the simple loops on each end of the beaded bead to finish the design.

5 Repeat steps 2–4 to create a second earring.

Materials

Earrings, 2¼ in. (5 cm)
- 1–2 g 11º seed beads, teal luster
- 1–2 g 11º cylinder beads, transparent blue gray rainbow luster
- **8** 4 mm bicone crystals, blue zircon
- **4** 4 mm bicone crystals, indicolite
- **16** 3 mm bicone crystals, indicolite
- **2** 10 mm helix crystals, crystal
- **2** 16 mm round glass pearls, light blue
- **2** 3 mm round glass pearls, light gray
- pair of earring hooks
- **2** 2-in. (5 cm) head pins
- **2** 2-in. eye pins
- tool kit, p. 71

Note: All findings are sterling silver.

Techniques

Starting a new thread, p. 74
Attaching a new thread, p. 74
Securing thread, p. 75
Making loops, p. 77

"Consider your work environment. I like to bead in a space that's clean and clutter-free because I have room to spread out. And there's something about blank white walls that helps me think freely."

Chemistry

One of the first pieces of jewelry I created used a seed bead stitch called the Dutch Spiral. This design takes inspiration from that technique to create a weave that's simple but striking, and totally different from plain bead weaving. I really enjoyed figuring out how to manipulate the beading wire into a spiral weave for a complex look.

Necklace

Spiral Rope

1 Cut a comfortable length of sterling silver beading thread, pick up two 3 mm cube beads, and pass up through the first cube bead. Pass down through the second cube bead, pick up an 8º seed bead and an 11ºseed bead, skip the 11º, and then go up through the 8º and the cube bead. Pick up an 8º and an 11º, skip the 11º, and pass down through the 8º and the cube bead to complete the top picot.

2 Pick up a cube bead and go down through the previous cube bead. Go up through the new cube bead and stitch a picot on the top and bottom of the cube bead **(figure 1)**. Continue stitching the cubes and picots together until you have a 7-in. (18 cm) band. Stitch a cube bead without picots and secure the thread.

3 Cut 2 yd. (1.8 m) of sterling silver beading wire and place a Bead Stopper at one end, leaving 1 in. (2 cm) for crimping. Pass the wire through the 11º of the first top picot. Pick up four 11ºs, a 3 mm bicone, and four 11ºs and go through the 11º of the first bottom picot. Then pick up a 2 mm crimp and go through the 11º of the second top picot in a clockwise motion **(figure 2)**. Crimp the crimp tube.

NOTE 12 in. (30 cm) of beading wire will allow for 1 in. (2.5 cm) of spiral rope. If you want a longer necklace, add a few extra feet of beading wire.

4 Repeat step 3, stringing the seed beads and crystal bicones as described, but increase the seed bead count after three or four stitches, and do not string a crimp tube after the first stitch.

5 For the last stitch, pick up a crimp tube before passing the wire through the 11º. Go through the 11º and then pick up four 11ºs, a 3 mm bicone, and four 11ºs, and go through the crimp tube. Create a flat crimp and trim the beading wire. Apply a crimp cover and repeat this step on the other side to finish the spiral rope.

6 Repeat steps 1–5 to create a second spiral rope.

Skill level: Beginner/intermediate

Materials
Necklace, 15 in. (38 cm)
- 7 g 11º seed beads, AB violet
- 7 g 8º seed beads, matte violet
- 7 g 3 mm cube beads, transparent violet
- **112** 3 mm bicone crystals, violet
- **12** 6 mm bicone crystals, violet
- **4** 14 mm rivoli crystals, violet
- 6 mm spacer
- toggle clasp
- **8** 6 mm jump rings
- **6** 2 mm crimp tubes
- **5** 4 mm crimp covers
- **4** 1-in. (2 cm) head pins
- 5.3 yd. (4.9 m) beading wire, .019, sterling silver
- tool kit, p. 71
Note: All findings are sterling silver.

Techniques
Starting a new thread, p. 74
Attaching a new thread, p. 74
Securing thread, p. 75
Flattened crimp, p. 76
Applying a crimp cover, p. 76
Making simple loops, p. 77
Opening and closing jump rings, p. 77

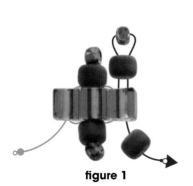

figure 1

figure 2

Pendant

1 Cut a comfortable length of beading thread and pick up two 11º seed beads, an 8º seed bead, and an 11º, and go through the first seed bead to form a loop. Pick up three 11ºs and an 8º, and go down through the second 11º added in the first loop and the second 11º in this stitch to complete the next loop (**figure 3**).

2 Stitch eight more loops until you have a total of 10. Join the ends to form a ring: Pick up two 11ºs and go up through the 11º of the first loop. Pick up an 8º and go down though the 11º of the last loop and through the second 11º of the new picot (**figure 4**). Pick up an 11º and go through the next 11º in the first loop.

3 Go through the seed beads until the thread exits to the right of the 8º, and turn the ring over. Pick up three 11ºs and go through the 8º to form a loop. Go through the first two seed beads again (**figure 5**) and stitch the remaining loops as in step 1, using the 8ºs of the previous loops. Insert the rivoli crystal between the two rows of loops before completing the last stitch. Complete the last stitch, and then secure the threads.

4 Repeat steps 1–3 to create three more pendants.

5 Cut 24 in. (61 cm) of sterling silver beading wire and place a Bead Stopper at one end, leaving a 4-in. (10 cm) tail. Pick up a 6 mm spacer, a crimp tube, a 6 mm bicone, a pendant (pass the wire through two of the 8ºs), and a 6 mm bicone. Go through the 6 mm spacer and crimp tube so that the wires cross each other. Adjust the wire loop so that it is about 1½ in. (3.8 cm) long. Pick up a 6 mm bicone, a pendant, a 6 mm bicone, a pendant, and a 6 mm bicone. Go through the crimp tube again, but make the loop slightly smaller than the first one. Create a third loop with one pendant with a 6 mm bicone on both sides, and make the loop smaller than the first two.

NOTE It may get crowded inside the crimp tube, so use your bentnose pliers to push the wire through the crimp tube. Also, you don't need to create a folded crimp because the tube is already very full.

6 Make sure the 6 mm spacer covers the crimp tube. Pick up a 6 mm bicone on both wires. Pick up a crimp tube on one of the wires and cross the other wire through the same crimp tube. Crimp the tubes, trim the wires, and apply a crimp cover.

7 Pick up a 6 mm bicone on a head pin and make a simple loop. Attach the simple loop to a jump ring and then attach the jump ring to the bottom of a pendant to create a small dangle. Repeat with all four pendants to complete the centerpiece.

figure 3

figure 4

figure 5

Assembling the Necklace

1 Attach a jump ring to each of the end cube beads of the spiral rope.

2 Attach a clasp to the jump ring on one end of the spiral rope. The other end will attach to the top loop of the centerpiece.

3 Repeat steps 1 and 2 to attach the second spiral rope on the other end of the necklace.

Bracelet

1 Create a 7-in. (18 cm) spiral rope following steps 1–5 of "Spiral Rope."

2 Attach a jump ring and clasp to both cube beads at the ends of the spiral rope to complete the design.

Materials

Bracelet, 8 in. (20 cm)
- 4 g 11º seed beads, AB violet
- 4 g 8º seed beads, matte violet
- 4 g 3 mm cube beads, transparent violet
- **56** 3 mm bicone crystals, violet
- toggle clasp
- **2** 6 mm jump rings
- **2** 2 mm crimp tubes
- **2** 4 mm crimp covers
- 2.3 yd. (2.1 m) beading wire, .019, sterling silver
- tool kit, p. 71

Note: All findings are sterling silver.

Techniques

Starting a new thread, p. 74
Attaching a new thread, p. 74
Securing thread, p. 75
Flattened crimp, p. 76
Applying a crimp cover, p. 76

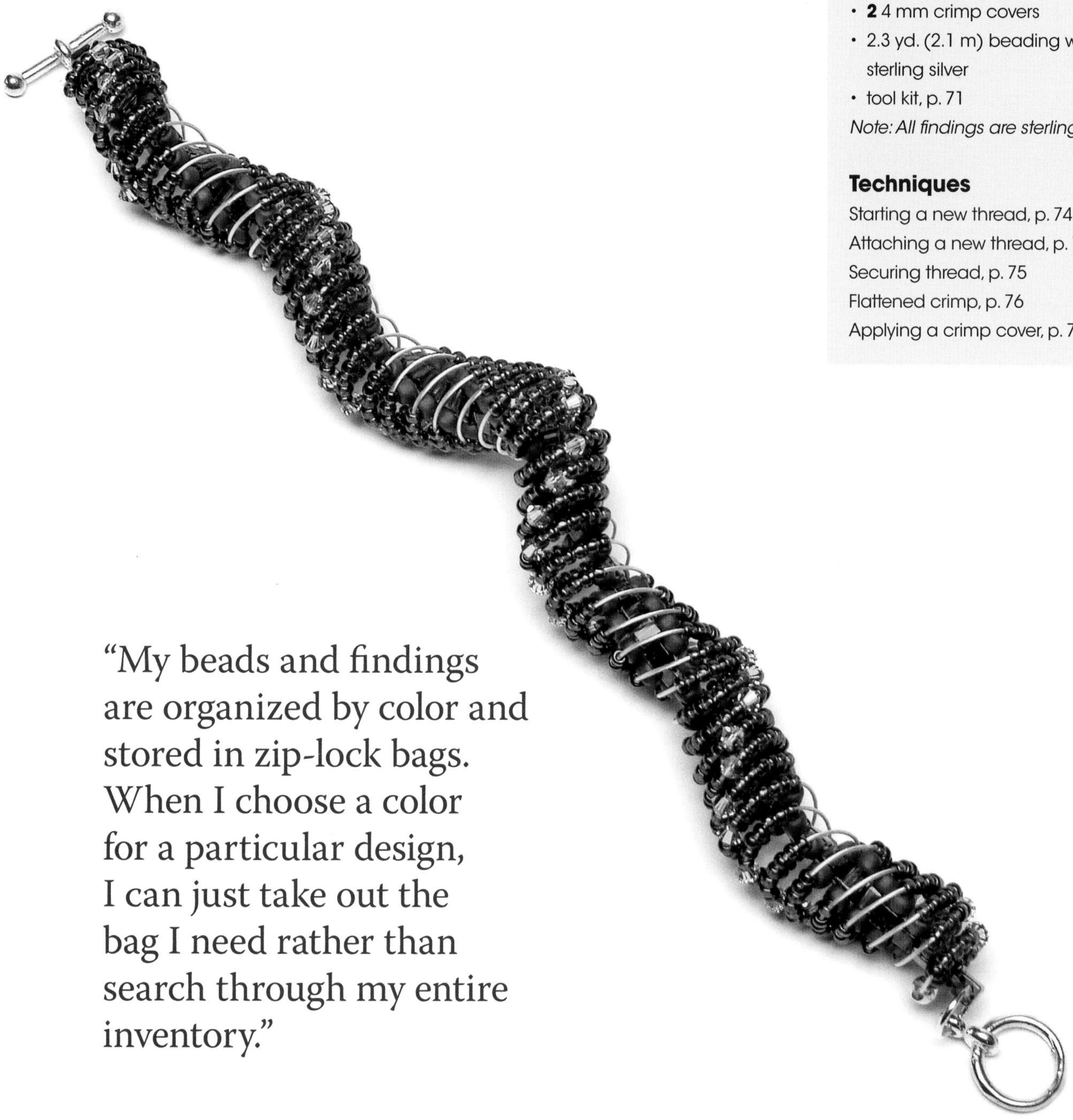

"My beads and findings are organized by color and stored in zip-lock bags. When I choose a color for a particular design, I can just take out the bag I need rather than search through my entire inventory."

Earrings

1 Create a pendant, following steps 1–4 of "Pendant," except use a total of 13 8°s stitched together to fit the 16 mm rivoli crystal.

2 Cut 2 in. (5 cm) of sterling silver beading wire and pick up a 6 mm bicone, the pendant (pass the wire through two of the 8°s), and a 6 mm bicone.

3 Gather both ends of the wire and pick up a clamshell and a crimp tube. Create a flattened crimp at the very top of the wires and close the clamshell. Attach the earring hooks to the clamshell hook.

4 Pick up a 6 mm bicone on a head pin and create a simple loop. Attach the simple loop to a jump ring and then attach the jump ring to an 8° at the bottom of the pendant to create a small dangle.

5 Repeat steps 1–4 to make a second earring.

Materials
Earrings, 2¼ in. (5.7 cm)
- 1 g 11° seed beads, AB violet
- 1 g 8° seed beads, matte violet
- **6** 6 mm bicone crystals, violet
- **2** 16 mm rivoli crystals, violet
- **2** 6 mm jump rings
- **2** 2 mm crimp tubes
- **2** 2 mm clamshells
- pair of earring hooks
- **2** 1-in. (2.5 cm) head pins
- 4 in. (10 cm) beading wire, .019, sterling silver
- beading toolkit, p. 71

Note: All findings are sterling silver.

Techniques
Starting a new thread, p. 74
Attaching a new thread, p. 74
Securing thread, p. 75
Folded crimp, p. 75
Attaching a clamshell, p. 76
Making simple loops, p. 77
Opening and closing jump rings, p. 77

"I always keep a sketchbook with me. I like to tape pictures, stick notes, write inspiring quotes, mark color swatches, and sketch designs in it. I can always refer back to my notes and inspiration when I need to come up with a new design."

Queen

I designed this set while I was at a friend's house. Sometimes you're hit with inspiration at the oddest times, but the idea came to me randomly while I was talking to my friend about my college classes. You never know when creative lightning will strike! This is a very airy and delicate design. I love the links that look like flowers, and the strong hit of color livens up any outfit.

Skill level: Beginner/intermediate

Materials
Necklace, 18 in. (46 cm)
- 5 g 15º seed beads, transparent violet luster
- 2 g 11º seed beads, silver-lined pink
- 5 g 11º triangle beads, silver-lined light amethyst
- 5 g 3 mm bugle beads, transparent pink
- **38** 4 mm bicone crystals, fuchsia
- **5** 3 mm bicone crystals, fuchsia
- **37** 3 mm round pearls, rosaline
- **35** 4 mm round pearls, rosaline
- **4** 6 mm round pearls, rosaline
- **2** 12 mm rivoli crystal, light rose
- **3** 14 mm rivoli crystal, light rose
- 2-loop box clasp
- **5** 1 mm crimp tubes
- **5** 1-in. (2 cm) head pins
- 24 in. (61 cm) 22-gauge half-hard wire
- 2 yd. (1.8 m) beading wire, .014, sterling silver
- tool kit, p. 71

Note: All findings are sterling silver.

Techniques
Starting a new thread, p. 74
Securing thread, p. 75
Flattened crimp, p. 76
Making simple loops, p. 77

Necklace

Crystal Flowers

1 Cut a comfortable length of beading thread and pick up a 3 mm bugle bead, a 15º seed bead, an 11º triangle bead, and a 15º, and go up through the bugle bead. Pick up a 15º, a triangle bead, and a 15º seed bead, and go up through the bugle bead again (**figure 1**).

2 Pick up two bugle beads, a 15º, a triangle bead, and a 15º, and repeat step 1 to stitch two bead loops to the second bugle bead. Repeat this step to stitch a total of 12 bugle beads together with six of the bugle beads having bead loops (this count will fit the 12 mm rivoli crystal). Go through the first bugle bead to complete the bead loop and then through a 15º and a triangle bead. Pick up three 15ºs and go though the next triangle bead of one of the beaded loops (**figure 2**). Stitch three 15ºs between each triangle bead to create the bottom casing. Stitch the remaining bugle beads in the same manner to create the front casing but before closing the last stitch, insert the 12 mm rivoli crystal.

3 Stitch back through the beads to get to the back side triangle bead. Pick up an 11º and go through the triangle bead again. Go through the three 15ºs and the next triangle and pick up another 11º. Repeat this for all the triangle beads on the back side, and then secure the threads.

4 Cut a 12-in. (30 cm) length of sterling silver beading wire and place a Bead Stopper 1 in. (2.5 cm) before the end.

5 Pass the wire though one of the 11ºs on the back of the crystal rivoli and pick up two 4 mm bicones. Pass the wire through the same 11º and gently pull to create a 10 mm loop.

6 Pass the wire through the next 11º and pick up a 4 mm bicone. Pass the wire though the 4 mm bicone of the previous loop, the 11º, and then through the next 11º to create a petal (**figure 3**).

7 Repeat step 6 five times for a total of 6 petals.

8 Remove the Bead Stopper and pick up a crimp tube. Cross the other wire through the crimp tube and flatten the crimp to secure. Trim the wires to complete the crystal flower.

9 Create another crystal flower using a 12 mm crystal rivoli and create three crystal flowers using 14 mm crystal rivolis.

NOTE The 14 mm crystal flower will have a total of 14 bugle beads stitched around the rivoli crystal. Seven of those bugle beads will have bead loops.

Assembling the Necklace

1 Create a simple loop at the end of the half-hard wire. Pick up a 4 mm round pearl and trim the wire ½ in. (1.3 cm) above the pearl. Create another simple loop to complete the pearl link.

2 Create 16 4 mm round pearl links and connect them together to create the pearl chain.

3 Create another pearl chain with 17 links using 3 mm round pearls.

4 Attach one end of the pearl chains to the box clasp and the other ends to two petals of the 12 mm crystal flower. Attach the two 14 mm crystal flowers and remaining 12 mm crystal flower with pearl links created from the 6 mm pearls and 4 mm pearls.

5 Repeat steps 1–4 for the other half of the necklace.

6 Pick up a 3 mm bicone on a head pin and create a simple loop. Using the remaining wire from the head pin, pick up a 4 mm bicone and make a loop on each side. Attach this link to the 3 mm link to create a dangle. Attach the dangle to the bottom crystal flower petal. Repeat for each of the five crystal flowers to complete the design.

figure 1

figure 2

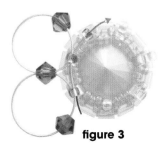

figure 3

Bracelet

1 Create four crystal flowers following steps 1–8 of "Crystal Flowers" and using 12 mm rivoli crystals.

2 Create 10 pearl links by making simple loops on each side of the 6 mm round pearls.

3 Attach the pearl links to the flower petals and the box clasp to finish the bracelet design.

Materials

Bracelet, 7½ in. (19 cm)

- 3 g 15º seed beads, transparent violet luster
- 2 g 11º seed beads, silver-lined pink
- 3 g 11º triangle beads, silver-lined light amethyst
- 3 g 3 mm bugle beads, transparent pink
- **24** 4 mm bicone crystals, fuchsia
- **10** 6 mm round pearls, rosaline
- **4** 12 mm rivoli crystal, light rose
- 2-loop filigree clasp
- **4** 1 mm crimp tubes
- 12 in. (30 cm) 22-gauge half-hard wire
- 4 ft. (1.2 m) beading wire, .014, sterling silver
- tool kit, p. 71

Note: All findings are sterling silver.

Techniques

Starting a new thread, p. 74
Securing thread, p. 75
Flattened crimp, p. 76
Making simple loops, p. 77

Materials

Earrings, 1½ in. (5 cm)

- 1 g 15º seed beads, transparent violet luster
- 1 g 11º seed beads, silver-lined pink
- 1 g 11º triangle beads, silver-lined light amethyst
- 1 g 3 mm bugle beads, transparent pink
- **12** 4 mm bicone crystals, fuchsia
- **2** 3 mm round pearls, rosaline
- **2** 4 mm round pearls, rosaline
- **2** 12 mm rivoli crystal, light rose
- pair of earring wires
- **2** 1 mm crimp tubes
- **2** 2-in. (5 cm) head pins
- 24 in. (61 cm) beading wire, .014, sterling silver
- tool kit, p. 71

Note: All findings are sterling silver.

Techniques

Starting a new thread, p. 74
Securing thread, p. 75
Flattened crimp, p. 76
Making simple loops, p. 77

Earrings

1 Create a crystal flower following steps 1–8 of "Crystal Flowers."

2 Pick up a 3 mm round pearl on a head pin and make a simple loop. Using the remaining wire from the head pin, pick up a 4 mm round pearl and make a simple loop on each side of the pearl. Attach one end to the 3 mm round pearl link and attach the other end to the bottom loop of the crystal flower.

3 Attach an earring wire to the top loop of the crystal flower.

4 Repeat steps 1–3 to create a second earring.

"I like to choose colors that tell a story and express the thought, emotion, or idea behind the design."

Sparkle

Sparkle was one of the first pieces I sketched for this collection. I wanted to create an airy lace pattern with lots of sparkle. Designing this piece was a challenge because I wanted to integrate a variety of textures without the beaded band becoming too busy. It's fun to make again and again in all the colors of the crystal rainbow!

Necklace

Beaded Picot Band

1 Start with a comfortable length of thread and pick up a 4 mm Pacific opal bicone, an 11º cylinder bead, two 8º seed beads, and a cylinder, and go up through the 4 mm bicone. Go through the top cylinder and down through the two 8ºs, and pick up a 4 mm cube bead. Go down through the two 8ºs again and up through the cube bead, and pick up an 8º. Go through the two 8ºs again and up through the cube bead, and pick up two 8ºs.

Skill level: Beginner/intermediate

Materials
Necklace, 14 in. (36 cm)
- 5–6 g 4 mm cube beads, metallic light blue
- 5 g 11º cylinder beads, transparent sea foam luster
- 7 g 8º seed beads, silver-lined alabaster
- **70** 3 mm bicone crystals, Indian sapphire
- **65** 4 mm bicone crystals, Pacific opal
- **60** 4 mm bicone crystals, Montana
- **32** 6 mm bicone crystals, Indian sapphire
- **5** 6 mm bicone crystals, Montana
- 2-loop slider clasp
- **8** 2-in. (28 cm) head pins
- **12** 6 mm jump rings
- **5** 2 mm crimp tubes
- **4** 4 mm crimp covers
- 3 in. (7.6 cm) jewelry chain, 6 mm links
- 5 in. (13 cm) jewelry chain, 2 mm links
- **2** 30 mm x 24 mm filigree pendants
- 3.3 yd. (3.0 m) beading wire, .014, antique brass
- tool kit, p. 71

Note: All findings are antique brass.

Techniques
Starting a new thread, p. 74
Attaching a new thread, p. 74
Securing thread, p. 75
Flattened crimp, p. 76
Applying a crimp cover, p. 76
Making simple loops, p. 77
Opening and closing jump rings, p. 77

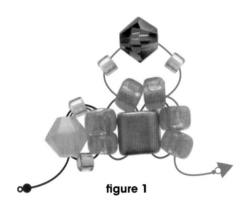

figure 1

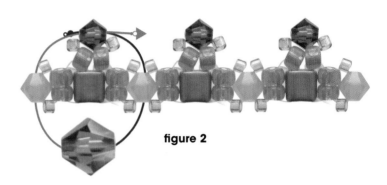

figure 2

"I work in a room that's dedicated to jewelry making: my studio. It can be stressful moving projects from place to place, and the room I use is well lit, organized, and inviting. If you don't have a room available, try finding a table that you can place in the brightest room of your home."

2 Go up through the cube bead and position the two seed beads to the right side of the cube. Pick up an 8º and go down the two 8ºs and up through the cube bead. Go through the top right 8º and pick up a cylinder, a 4 mm Montana bicone, and a cylinder bead. Go clockwise through the top two 8ºs, then down through the right two 8ºs (**figure 1**). Pick up a cylinder, a 4 mm Pacific opal bicone, and a cylinder, and go down through the two 8ºs then through the bottom cylinder, and up through the 4 mm Pacific opal bicone.

3 Pick up a cylinder bead, two 8ºs, and a cylinder bead, and go up through the 4 mm Pacific opal bicone. Repeat steps 1 and 2 to create the beaded band. Make a total of 30 picots to create a 15-in. (38 cm) band, and then secure the threads.

4 Follow steps 1–3 to create a second beaded picot band.

Weaving the Beading Wire

1 Cut 1.67 yd. (1.5 m) of antique brass beading wire, crimp one end, and apply a crimp cover. Pass the beading wire clockwise through the first 4 mm Montana bicone and down through the next 4 mm Pacific opal bicone. Pick up a 6 mm Indian sapphire bicone and pass up through the previous 4 mm Pacific opal bicone, and then through the top 4 mm Montana bicone again (**figure 2**).

2 Pass the wire through the next 4 mm Montana bicone and repeat the weaving technique for the remainder of the beaded picot band. Place a Bead Stopper on the end of the wire and set the beadwork aside.

3 Cut 1.67 yd. of beading wire and weave it through the second beaded picot band using the same weaving technique, except weave through the already woven 6 mm Indian sapphire bicones of the previous band to join the two bands (**figure 3**).

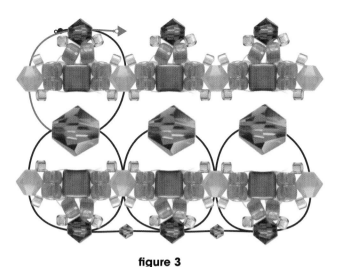

figure 3

4 After the last weave, adjust the tension of the wire loops if they are too tight or too loose, and crimp the beading wire right next to the last 4 mm Montana bicone. Trim the excess wire and apply a crimp cover.

Wire Flourish Pendant

1 Cut 1.67 yd. of beading wire and place a Bead Stopper 1 in. (2.5 cm) from one end. Go up through one of the holes in the filigree pendant and pick up a 4 mm golden crystal shadow bicone. Go down through another hole of the filigree and leave a 1-in. loop. Go up through another hole and repeat the weaving to create the flourishes, randomly picking up 6 mm and 4 mm Montana crystals and 6 mm Indian sapphire bicones as you weave the loops. The end of the wire should be on the back side of the pendant. Leave at least an inch of wire for crimping.

2 Remove the Bead Stopper from the wire and pick up a crimp tube. Cross the other wire through the crimp tube and crimp. Trim the excess wire and pull on the wire loops to adjust the flourishes.

3 Attach the second filigree pendant to the back of the flourish pendant by passing two head pins (one at each end) through both filigree pendants and creating a P-shaped loop on the back **(figure 4)**. Attach six 6 mm jump rings to the bottom of the pendants by passing them through the filigree holes.

4 Use the jewelry chain to create fringe: Cut the chain into various lengths and attach 4 mm bicones and 4 mm cube beads between the chain links and the chain ends. Attach the beaded chains to the jump rings at the bottom of the wire flourish pendant to finish.

figure 4

NOTE Recycle your head pins: Create a simple loop on one end, pick up a 4 mm bicone, and then make another simple loop. Connect the simple loops together to create a beaded chain. You can make as much beaded chain as you like.

Assembling the Necklace

1 Attach the wire flourish pendant to the middle of the beaded picot band by slightly opening the P-loops on the back of the pendant and inserting the beading wire (on the edge of the band) into it.

2 Attach a 6 mm jump ring on both sides of the 4 mm Montana bicone of the last wire loops. Attach the slide clasp to those jump rings to finish the necklace.

Materials

Bracelet, 7 in. (18 cm)

- 4–5 g 4 mm cube beads, metallic light blue
- 4 g 11º cylinder beads, transparent sea foam luster
- 3 g 8º seed beads, silver-lined alabaster
- **24** 3 mm bicone crystals, Indian sapphire
- **28** 4 mm bicone crystals, Pacific opal
- **26** 4 mm bicone crystals, Montana
- **13** 6 mm bicone crystals, Indian sapphire
- 2-loop slider clasp
- **8** 6 mm jump rings
- **4** 2 mm crimp tubes
- **4** 4 mm crimp covers
- 2.67 yd. (2.4 m) beading wire, .014, antique brass
- tool kit, p. 71

Note: All findings are antique brass.

Techniques

Starting a new thread, p. 74
Attaching a new thread, p. 74
Securing thread, p. 75
Flattened crimp, p. 76
Applying a crimp cover, p. 76
Opening and closing jump rings, p. 77

Bracelet

1 Create two 7-in. (18 cm) beaded picot bands (approximately 14 picots) following steps 1–3 of "Beaded Picot Band."

2 Cut two 24-in. (61 cm) pieces of antique brass beading wire and repeat steps 1–4 of "Weaving the Beading Wire."

3 Attach a jump ring on each side of the 4 mm Pacific opal bicones on the last wire loops. Attach the loops of the slide clasp to those jump rings to finish the bracelet.

Earrings

1 Pick up a filigree spacer on the eye pin and make a simple loop close to the spacer. Attach a jump ring on each side, and attach an earring hook to one of the jump rings.

2 Use the jewelry chain to create fringe: Cut the chain into various lengths, and attach a 4 mm Pacific opal bicone between the chain links and the chain ends. Attach the beaded chains to the empty jump ring at the bottom of the earring.

Flourish Spacer Bead

1 Cut 24 in. (61 cm) of beading wire and place a Bead Stopper 1 in. (2.5 cm) from one end. Go through one of the holes in the filigree spacer and pick up a 4 mm Montana bicone. Go through another hole and leave a ½-in. (1.3 cm) loop in the wire. Go through another hole and repeat the weaving to create flourishes around the spacer, randomly picking up 4 mm bicones and 6 mm bicones as the loops are woven. Leave 1 in. of wire for crimping.

2 Remove the Bead Stopper from the wire and pick up a crimp tube. Cross the other wire through the crimp tube and crimp. Trim the excess wire, pull on the wire loops to adjust the loops, and then apply a crimp cover to finish the earring.

3 Repeat to make a second earring.

Materials

Earrings, 2½ in. (6 cm)
- **12** 3 mm bicone crystals, Indian sapphire
- **14** 4 mm bicone crystals, Pacific opal
- **10** 4 mm bicone crystals, Montana
- **4** 6 mm bicone crystals, Indian sapphire
- **2** 6 mm filigree beads
- pair of earring hooks
- **2** 2 in. (5 cm) eye pins
- **4** 6 mm jump rings
- **2** 2 mm crimp tubes
- **2** 4 mm crimp covers
- 3 in. (8 cm) jewelry chain, 6 mm links
- 5 in. (13 cm) jewelry chain, 2 mm links
- 4 ft. (1.2 m) beading wire, .014, antique brass
- tool kit, p. 71

Note: All findings are antique brass.

Techniques

Flattened crimp, p. 76
Applying a crimp cover, p. 76
Making loops, p. 77
Opening and closing jump rings, p. 77

"Take plenty of breaks. Constantly sitting is bad for your posture and back, and working for a long period of time can cause eyestrain."

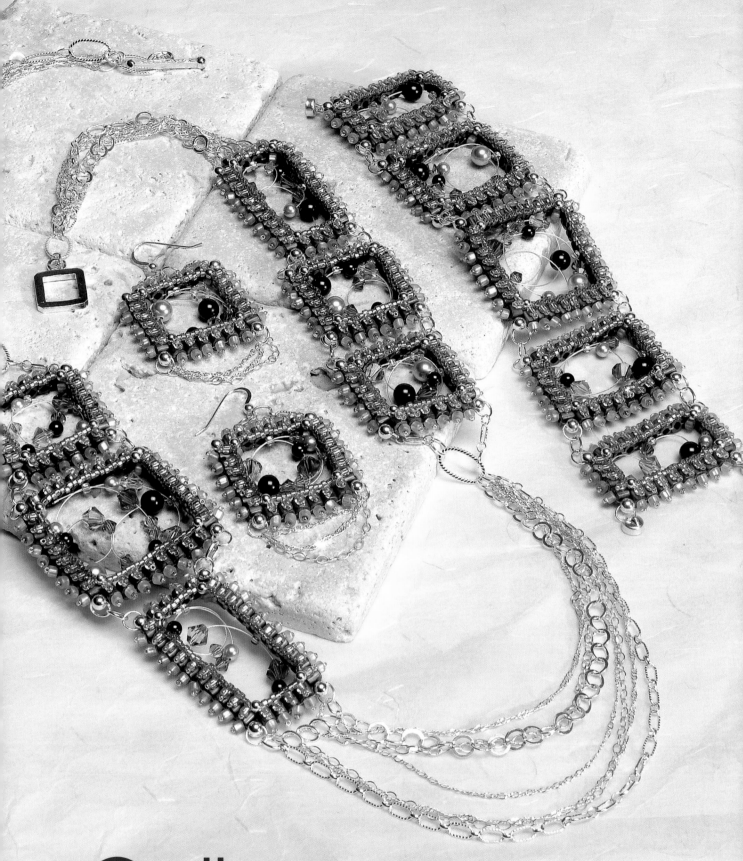

Gallery

I'll admit I never really had an affinity for abstract art, but I was pulled into it with this design. Gallery was inspired through the idea of controlled free form, In this project, you'll create a beaded frame and use beading wire to create "paint strokes." The bright crystals add splashes of color inside the airy canvases. As a bonus, the crystals move inside the frame to create a new picture every time you wear it. I really had fun with this piece and I hope you do, too!

Skill level: Beginner/intermediate

Materials
Necklace, 26 in. (66 cm)
- 3–5 g 15º seed beads, transparent rainbow gray
- 5 g 11º cylinder beads, transparent rainbow gray
- 5 g 8º triangle beads, silver-lined matte gold luster
- 30 g 4 mm cube beads, matte metallic blue gray
- **6** 4 mm round pearls, light blue
- **10** 4 mm round pearls, dark blue
- **3** 6 mm round pearls, light blue
- **4** 6 mm round pearls, dark blue
- **9** 4 mm bicone crystals, sapphire
- **7** 4 mm bicone crystals, light sapphire
- **5** 6 mm bicone crystals, sapphire
- **7** 6 mm bicone crystals, light sapphire
- **24** 3 mm round spacer
- **24** 4 mm round spacer
- **24** 5.5 mm jump rings
- **8** 3 mm x 5 mm jump rings
- **36** 6 mm x 12 mm chain links
- **6** 1 mm crimp tubes
- toggle clasp
- 2 yd. (1.8 m) beading wire, .014, sterling silver
- **5** assorted jewelry chains in 2-ft. (61 cm) lengths
- tool kit, p. 71

Note: All findings are sterling silver.

Techniques
Starting a new thread, p. 74
Securing thread, p. 75
Attaching a new thread, p. 74
Flattened crimp, p. 76
Opening and closing jump rings, p. 77

Necklace

Beaded Crystal Frame

1 Cut a comfortable length of beading thread and pick up a 4 mm cube bead, an 8º seed bead, and a 15º seed bead. Skip the 15º, go down through the 8º and the cube bead, and pick up an 8º triangle bead. Go down through the cube bead again so that the triangle bead sits on top of the cube bead. Pick up another cube bead and go down through the first cube bead to make a picot stitch (**figure 1**).

2 Go up through the new cube bead and repeat the picot stitch. Stitch two more cube beads together. Stitch the fifth cube bead, but pick up a triangle bead before going up through the fifth cube bead to stitch the picot (**figure 2**). Stitch three more cube beads together for a total of eight cube beads stitched together, with triangle bead below the fourth and fifth cube bead.

3 To create a corner, pick up an 8º, a cube bead, and a 4 mm spacer. Go down though the last cube bead in the previous stitch, and then go through the 8º and the new cube bead (**figure 3**). Continue stitching the picots and cube beads together as in the previous row, including the triangle bead below the cube beads to create a square with eight cube beads on each side. Secure the threads.

4 Start with a comfortable length of thread and go up through one of the triangle beads on top of a cube bead. Pick up a 15º and go down through the triangle bead again. Pick up two cylinders and go up through the next triangle bead. Repeat this stitch for the remaining triangles, but when you arrive at the corner, pick up a 3 mm spacer before going through the next triangle bead.

5 Stitch a cylinder between each set of two cylinders with the remaining thread. When you arrive at a corner, go through the 3 mm spacer and the cylinders before picking up another cylinder (**figure 4**). Secure the threads to complete the frame.

6 Cut 12 in. (30 cm) of sterling silver beading wire, and flatten a crimp 1 in. (2.5 cm) from one end. Pass through one of the triangle beads underneath the cube beads and randomly pick up one or two bicones or pearls. Pass through another triangle bead and pick up more bicones and pearls as desired (**figure 5**). Repeat until most of the wire is used up, then flatten a crimp tube and trim the wire if necessary.

NOTE It may be easier to work step 6 on the back of the frame because you can see the triangle beads more easily.

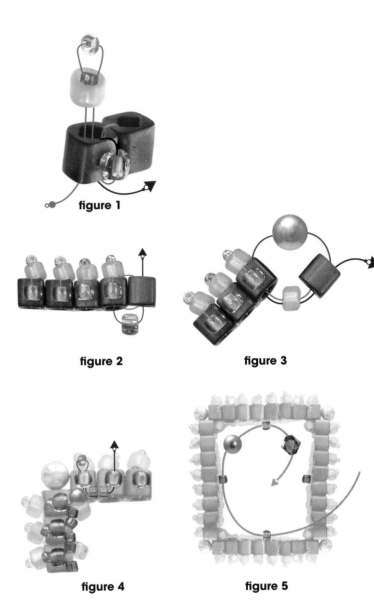

figure 1

figure 2

figure 3

figure 4

figure 5

7 After creating the large square frame, create three small square beaded frames that have six cube beads on each side. Create two rectangular beaded frames that are four cube beads in width by eight cube beads tall.

Assembling the Necklace

1 Attach a 5.5 mm jump ring to each corner spacer of the beaded frames and connect a large square frame, a small square frame, and a rectangular frame together (with the large frame between the other two frames, and the small frame on top) using 3 mm x 5 mm jump rings. Attach the two small frames and the second rectangular frame together using 3 mm x 5 mm jump rings.

2 Position the connected frames so the rectangular frame is connected to the large square frame on the left side and the rectangular frame that is connected to the two small squares is on the right side of the large square frame.

3 Cut a 1-in. piece of jewelry chain and attach each end to a corner jump ring of the rectangle frames. Cut two ½-in. (1.3 cm) pieces, and attach them to the jump rings of the square beaded frames. Attach a 3 mm x 5 mm jump ring to the chain ends and then to a 6 mm x 12 mm chain link. Repeat this step to attach the chains for the other rectangular and square frames.

4 Cut six 4-in. (10 cm) pieces of the assorted chains. Attach two of the chains to the corner jump rings of the rectangular frame and attach the four remaining chains to the chain across the rectangular frame using 3 mm x 5 mm jump rings. Gather the six chains and attach two 3 mm x 5 mm jump rings (three chains per jump ring) and attach them to a 6 mm x 12 mm chain link. Attach the chain link to a clasp with a 3 mm x 5 mm jump ring.

5 Use the remaining chain to create a drape between the small square frame and the rectangular frame. The chains will connect the same way as in step 4.

6 Connect the remaining 6 mm x 12 mm chain links together using two 3 mm x 5 mm jump rings. Attach a clasp to finish the necklace.

Bracelet

1 Create a large square frame with eight cube beads stitched together on each side following steps 1–6 of "Beaded Crystal Frames." Use the same stitch to create two rectangle frames that are six cube beads in width by eight cube beads tall and two rectangular frames that are four cube beads in width by eight cube beads tall. Make sure to stitch a triangle bead below the cube beads when stitching the cube beads together.

2 Attach a 5.5 mm jump ring to each corner spacer of the beaded frame, and connect the frames together with a 3 mm x 5 mm jump ring.

3 Attach the magnetic clasp to the end jump rings to finish the bracelet design.

Materials
Bracelet, 7½ in. (19 cm)
- 3–5 g 15º seed beads, transparent rainbow gray
- 5 g 11º cylinder beads, transparent rainbow gray
- 5 g 8º triangle beads, silver-lined matte gold luster
- 30 g 4 mm cube beads, matte metallic blue gray
- **7** 4 mm round pearls, light blue
- **3** 4 mm round pearls, dark blue
- **2** 6 mm round pearls, light blue
- **5** 6 mm round pearls, dark blue
- **6** 4 mm bicone crystals, sapphire
- **8** 4 mm bicone crystals, light sapphire
- **3** 6 mm bicone crystals, sapphire
- **3** 6 mm bicone crystals, light sapphire
- **20** 3 mm round spacer
- **20** 4 mm round spacer
- **20** 5.5 mm jump rings
- **8** 3 mm x 5 mm jump rings
- **5** 1 mm crimp tubes
- **2** magnetic clasps
- 1.67 yd. (1.5 m) beading wire, .014, sterling silver
- tool kit, p. 71

Note: All findings are sterling silver.

Techniques
Starting a new thread, p. 74
Attaching a new thread, p. 74
Securing thread, p. 75
Flattened crimp, p. 76
Opening and closing jump rings, p. 77

Earrings

1 Create a square woven crystal frame with six cube beads stitched together on each side following steps 1–6 of "Woven Crystal Frames."

2 Attach a 5.5 mm jump ring to each corner spacer. Cut 1-in. (2.5 cm), 1½-in. (3.8 cm), and 2-in. (5 cm) pieces of fine jewelry chain and attach to the bottom jump rings.

3 Cut two ½-in. (1.3 cm) lengths of chain and attach them to the jump rings at the top two corners of the beaded frame. Then attach a 3 mm x 5 mm jump ring to each chain end. Gather both chains together, and attach them to an earring hook to finish.

4 Repeat steps 1–3 to make a second earring.

Materials

Earrings, 2¼ in. (6 cm)

- 1–2 g 15º seed beads, transparent rainbow gray
- 1–2 g 11º cylinder beads, transparent rainbow gray
- 1–2 g 8º triangle beads, silver-lined matte gold luster
- 5 g 4 mm cube beads, matte metallic blue gray
- **2** 4 mm round pearls, light blue
- **2** 4 mm round pearls, dark blue
- **2** 6 mm round pearls, light blue
- **2** 6 mm round pearls, dark blue
- **4** 4 mm bicone crystals, sapphire
- **2** 4 mm bicone crystals, light sapphire
- **2** 6 mm bicone crystals, sapphire
- **2** 6 mm bicone crystals, light sapphire
- **8** 3 mm round spacer
- **8** 4 mm round spacer
- **8** 5.5 mm jump rings
- **4** 6 mm x 12 mm chain links
- **2** 1 mm crimp tubes
- pair of earring hooks
- 24 in. (61 cm) beading wire, .014, sterling silver
- **4** assorted jewelry chains in 6-in. (15 cm) lengths
- tool kit, p. 71

Note: All findings are sterling silver.

Techniques

Starting a new thread, p. 74
Securing thread, p. 75
Flattened crimp, p. 76
Opening and closing jump rings, p. 77

> "I like to work in short sessions before finding something else to do to refresh my mind."

Golden Nights

Golden Nights is the most unusual piece in this collection of jewelry designs because of its many layers and detailed, wired look. I sketched several different versions of this design, which I eventually combined after I started to bead. I like the juxtaposition of the metallic jump rings and spacers, and the soft gold beading wire that gives the illusion of space between the pearls.

Skill level: Intermediate

Materials

Necklace, 20 in. (51 cm)

- 5 g 11º seed beads, gold
- 5 g 11º cylinder beads, metallic dark green
- 10 g 8º seed beads, transparent light green AB
- **28** 4 mm bicone crystals, lime
- **14** 6 mm bicone crystals, lime
- **28** 4 mm bicone crystals, jonquil
- **14** 6 mm bicone crystals, jonquil
- **63** 4 mm round spacers
- **14** 12mm round pearls, light green
- toggle clasp
- **84** 9 mm jump rings
- **2** 2 mm crimp tubes
- **12** 1 mm crimp tubes
- **14** 4 mm crimp covers
- 10 ft. (3.0 m) beading wire, .014, 24k gold
- 1 yd. (.9 m) beading wire, .014
- tool kit, p. 71

Note: All findings are gold-filled.

Techniques

Starting a new thread, p. 74
Securing thread, p. 75
Folded crimp, p. 75
Flattened crimp, p. 76
Applying a crimp cover, p. 76
Opening and closing jump rings, p. 77
Making jump rings, p. 77

Necklace

Stringing the Necklace

1 Cut a 3-ft. (.9 m) piece of beading wire and place a Bead Stopper at one end. String the following pattern: two 8º seed beads, a 12 mm pearl, two 8ºs, a 4 mm jonquil bicone, an 11º seed bead, a 6 mm jonquil bicone, a 11º, and a 4 mm jonquil bicone 13 times. End with a pearl and two 8ºs.

2 String a 4 mm jonquil bicone and place a Bead Stopper on each end.

Beaded Bead Caps

1 Cut a comfortable length of beading thread and go down through the first two 8ºs of the strung necklace. Pick up an 8º and go through the second 8º. Repeat this five more times so that six 8ºs are stitched around the core 8º.

2 Go up through an 8º added in the previous step. Pick up an 11º cylinder bead. Go down through the 8º to the left, pick up an 8º, and go up through the first 8º. Pick up an 11º **(figure 1)**. Go through the 8º added in the previous stitch, back through the 11º, and down through the 8º on the left **(figure 2)** to complete the stitch.

3 Pick up an 8º and go up through the next 8º on the left. Pick up a cylinder bead and go down through the previous 8º on the right, through the bottom 8º, and up through the left 8º. Pick up an 11º and go through the bottom 8º from left to right and then from right to left through the 11º. Go down through the previous 8º, through the bottom 8º, and up through the left 8º to start the next stitch.

4 Use steps 2 and 3 alternatively to complete the beaded bead caps, and go through the core 8º, the pearl, and the first 8º to make another bead cap on the other side of the pearl. You may have to rotate the necklace so that you are more comfortable stitching the second bead cap.

5 After the second bead cap is finished, pass through the crystals to stitch the remaining beaded bead caps on both sides of the pearls only.

6 After stitching all the bead caps, crimp the ends of the beading wire to the clasp and close a crimp cover over the crimp.

Attaching the Jump Rings

Place three 9 mm jump rings on the bottom 8ºs of the bead cap. Skip an 8º between each jump ring and attach a 4 mm spacer to each of those jump rings. Repeat this step for the bottom bead cap, except go through the 4 mm spacer attached to the top bead cap before closing the jump ring **(figure 3)**. Repeat for all of the pearls on the necklace. Tuck the seam of the jump ring inside the spacer to finish the necklace.

NOTE A specific size of jump rings can be hard to find, so you can make them instead. Use a spool of 22-gauge half-hard wire, and coil it around a pen. Cut the coil using your double-flush cutters and you'll instantly have jump rings.

Woven Crystal Cluster

1 Cut 12 in. (30 cm) of 24k gold beading wire and place a Bead Stopper 1 in. (2.5 cm) from the end. In a clockwise motion, go through an 11º of the bottom bead cap of the beaded pearl and top bead cap 11ºs of the next beaded pearl, occasionally picking up a spacer bead or a 4 mm khaki bicone **(figure 4)**. Each cluster uses four 4 mm khaki bicones and two spacer beads.

2 Remove the Bead Stopper and string a 1 mm crimp. Cross both wires inside the crimp tube and crimp. Trim the excess wire and apply a crimp cover to finish the woven crystal cluster. Repeat to create a crystal cluster between every other beaded pearl to finish the necklace.

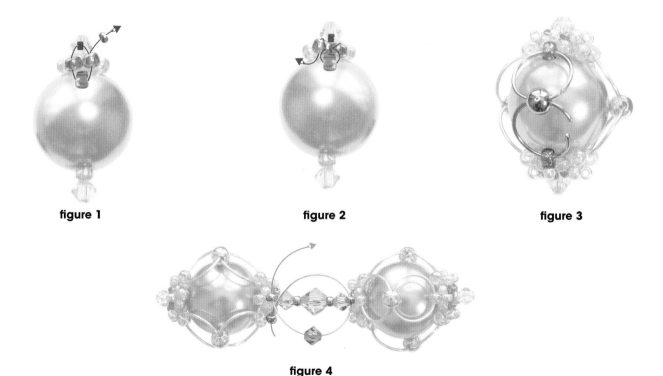

figure 1

figure 2

figure 3

figure 4

Bracelet

1 Place a Bead Stopper at one end of a comfortable length of beading wire and string a pattern of an 11º seed bead, three 8º seed beads, a 12 mm round pearl, three 8ºs, an 11º, and a 6 mm jonquil bicone. Repeat this pattern five more times, and finish the bracelet on each end with a 4 mm jonquil crystal. Place Bead Stoppers at each end.

2 Stitch the beaded bead caps to all the pearls and secure the bracelet following steps 1–6 of "Beaded Bead Caps."

3 Attach the jump rings around the pearls following "Attaching the Jump Rings" to complete the bracelet.

4 Create the woven crystal clusters between the pearls following steps 1 and 2 of "Woven Crystal Clusters," but omit the two 6 mm lime bicones.

Materials

Bracelet, 7½ in. (19 cm)

- 2–5 g 11º seed beads, gold
- 2–5 g 8º seed beads, transparent light green AB
- 5 g 11º cylinder beads, metallic dark green
- **12** 4 mm bicone crystals, lime
- **8** 6 mm bicone crystals, lime
- **10** 4 mm bicone crystals, jonquil
- **6** 6 mm bicone crystals, jonquil
- **28** 4 mm round spacers
- **5** 12 mm round pearls, light green
- toggle clasp
- **30** 9 mm jump rings
- **4** 1 mm crimp tubes
- **2** 2 mm crimp tubes
- **6** 4 mm crimp covers
- 5 ft. (1.5 m) beading wire, .014, 24k gold
- 12 in. (30 cm) beading wire, .014
- tool kit, p. 71

Note: All findings are gold-filled.

Techniques

Starting a new thread, p. 74
Securing thread, p. 75
Folded crimp, p. 75
Flattened crimp, p. 76
Applying a crimp cover, p. 76
Opening and closing jump rings, p. 77

Earrings

1 On a head pin, string a 4 mm jonquil bicone, an 8º seed bead, a 4 mm jonquil bicone, an 11º seed bead, a 6 mm jonquil bicone, an 11º, a 4 mm jonquil bicone, an 8º, and a 4 mm jonquil bicone. Place a Bead Stopper at the end.

2 Stitch two bead caps on each of the 8ºs on the head pin following steps 1–4 of "Beaded Bead Caps."

NOTE Start with the top 8º when creating the first bead cap. After completing the first bead cap, stitch an 8º between each of the bottom 8ºs and repeat for the second bead cap.

3 Create a woven crystal cluster following steps 1 and 2 of "Woven Crystal Clusters."

4 Repeat steps 1–3 to make a second earring.

Materials
Earrings, 1½ in. (4 cm)
- 1 g 11º seed beads, gold
- 1 g 8º seed beads, transparent light green AB
- 1 g 11º cylinder beads, metallic dark green
- **8** 4 mm bicone crystals, lime
- **4** 6 mm bicone crystals, lime
- **8** 4 mm bicone crystals, jonquil
- **2** 6 mm bicone crystals, jonquil
- **4** 4 mm round spacers
- pair of earring hooks
- **2** 2 mm crimp tubes
- **2** 4 mm crimp covers
- 2 2-in. (5 cm) head pins
- 24 in. (61 cm) beading wire, .014, 24k gold
- tool kit, p. 71

Note: All findings are gold-filled.

Techniques
Starting a new thread, p. 74
Securing thread, p. 75
Flattened crimp, p. 76
Applying a crimp cover, p. 76
Opening and closing jump rings, p. 77

"I keep a cork board near my workspace. I usually pin up my patterns, sketches, or materials on the board for easy access, clutter control, and convenience. A marker board is also great for posting reminders or a bead shopping list."

Sunshine Lady

This cheerful piece was inspired by an old Edwardian jewelry design I saw in an art book. I finished the garland rope before actually designing the piece; an added sunflower pendant complements the concept of happiness—and looks and feels extravagant.

Skill level: Advanced

Materials

Necklace, 25 in. (64 cm)

- 10 g 8º seed beads, silver-lined matte dark gold luster
- 10 g 11º seed beads, transparent gold luster
- 10 g 11º seed beads, matte brown iris
- 10 g 11º seed beads, silver-lined matte gold luster
- 3 g 15º seed beads, transparent gold luster
- **207** 3 mm bicone crystals, crystal golden shadow
- **7** 4 mm bicone crystals, crystal golden shadow
- 14 mm rivoli crystal, crystal golden shadow
- **3** 4 mm spacer beads
- **2** 5 mm spacer beads
- toggle clasp
- **4** 4 mm jump rings
- **4** 2 mm crimp tubes
- **6** 1 mm crimp tubes
- **6** 4 mm crimp covers
- 12 in. (30 cm) beading wire, .014, 24k gold
- 12 in. beading wire, .018, antique brass
- 1 yd. (.9 m) beading wire, .014
- tool kit, p. 71

Note: All findings are gold-filled.

Techniques

Starting a new thread, p. 74
Securing thread, p. 75
Folded crimp, p. 75
Applying a crimp cover, p. 76
Making simple loops, p. 77
Opening and closing jump rings, p. 77

Necklace

Garland Rope

1 Cut 18 in. (46 cm) of beading wire and crimp one end to a jump ring. Apply a crimp cover and pick up a pattern of five 11º matte brown iris seed beads and an 8º seed bead 25 times to create a 10-in. (25 cm) rope. Place a Bead Stopper at the end.

figure 1

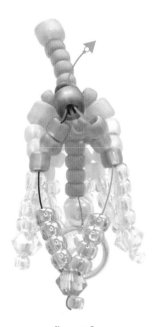

figure 2

2 Cut a comfortable length of beading thread and go up through the first 8º strung on the wire. Pick up an 11º matte brown iris, an 8º, and an 11º matte brown iris and go up through the 8º on the wire again. Repeat three more times.

3 Go down through the first set of beads stitched in step 1, and exit through the 8º. Pick up three 11º silver-lined matte gold luster seed beads, four 11º transparent gold luster seed beads, a 3 mm bicone, and a 15º seed bead. Skip the 15º, go up through the 3 mm bicone, and pick up four 11º transparent gold lusters and three 11º silver-lined matte gold lusters. Go up through the 8º and the 11º matte brown iris on top (**figure 1**).

4 Go down though the next top 11º matte brown iris and the 8º, and pick up two 11º silver-lined matte gold lusters. Pass down through the third 11º silver-lined matte gold luster of the previous beaded loop and pick up four 11º transparent gold lusters, a 3 mm bicone, and a 15º. Skip the 15º, go up through the 3 mm bicone, and pick up four 11º transparent gold lusters and three 11º silver-lined matte gold lusters. Go up through the 8º and the 11º on top (**figure 2**). Repeat this step to complete a third beaded loop.

5 Begin the fourth beaded loop as in step 4, but stop after picking up the second set of four 11º transparent gold lusters. Go up through the third 11º silver-lined matte gold luster of the first beaded loop created in step 3. Pick up two 11º silver-lined matte gold lusters and go up through the 8º and the 11º on top (**figure 3**). You have completed one beaded floret.

6 Go down through the next five 11º matte brown irises and the 8º on the wire and create another beaded floret after the last floret as in step 3–5. Continue in this manner for the length of the beads on the wire. Secure the threads and remove the Bead Stopper. Crimp a jump ring to the end of the wire and attach one half of the clasp to the jump ring to finish the garland rope.

7 Repeat steps 1–6 to create a second garland rope.

figure 3

Sunflower Pendant

1 On a comfortable length of beading thread, pick up an 11º silver-lined matte gold luster and an 8º seed bead. Go through the 11º again to make a loop. Pick up an 11º matte brown iris, go though the 8º, and then pick up another 11º matte brown iris and go through the 11º silver-lined matte gold luster (**figure 4**). Go up through the 11º matte brown iris, pick up an 8º and a 11º silver-lined matte gold luster, and go through the 11º matte brown iris seed bead in the previous stitch. Go through the 8º and pick up an 11º matte brown iris. Go through the 11º silver-lined matte gold luster and the 8º again. Then go down through the 11º matte brown iris (**figure 5**).

2 Continue as in step 1 until 13 8ºs are stitched together. Close the beaded circle by picking up an 11º matte brown iris and going up through the first 11º silver-lined matte gold luster. Pick up an 8º and go through the 11º silver-lined matte gold luster again. Go though the 11º matte brown iris and stitch an 11º transparent gold luster between each 11º silver-lined matte gold luster.

3 Go up through the next 11º matte brown iris and pick up two 11º silver-lined matte gold lusters and eight 15ºs.

4 Go up through the fourth 11º matte brown iris and pick up two 11º silver-lined matte gold lusters and six 15ºs, and go down through the second 11º matte brown iris (**figure 6**).

5 Pick up two 11º silver-lined matte gold lusters and eight 15ºs, and repeat step 4 for the remaining 11º matte brown irises.

6 Insert the 14 mm rivoli crystal when you are nearly finished with the beaded casing, and stitch under the previous beading so that the spiral looks continuous. Secure the threads after the beaded rivoli crystal is finished.

figure 4   **figure 5**

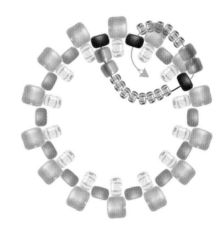

figure 6

figure 7

7 Place a Bead Stopper at the end of a comfortable length of gold beading wire and pass it through one of the 8°s in the beaded rivoli crystal. Pick up a spacer and pass it through the 8° again and pull the wire to form a ¾ in. (1 cm) loop. Repeat this step for every other 8° and pick up random spacers as you construct the petals. Remove the Bead Stopper and pick up a crimp tube. Pass the other wire through the crimp tube so the wires cross and create a folded crimp. Trim the excess wires and apply a crimp cover.

8 Repeat step 7 to create the second layer of petals using antique brass beading wire, except make the loops 1 in. (2.5 cm).

9 Gently run the first notch of the crimping pliers along both wires of the petal to create a pointed tip **(figure 7)**. Repeat this step for all the petals to finish the sunflower pendant.

Assembling the Necklace
Attach the jump ring of the garland rope to the sunflower pendant.

"I store finished projects in small zip-lock bags that are then placed in a mid-sized plastic container. This keeps the precious metals from tarnishing and the beads from scratching other beads."

Bracelet

1 Cut a 6-in. (15 cm) length of beading wire and crimp a jump ring at one end. Pick up a pattern of five 11º matte brown iris seed beads and an 8º seed bead seven times. Place a Bead Stopper at the end and follow steps 2–6 of "Garland Rope."

2 Create a sunflower pendant following steps 1–8 of "Sunflower Pendant," except make the wire loops ½ in. (1.3 cm) to create smaller flower petals.

3 Attach the garland rope jump ring to the flower petal to complete the bracelet.

Materials

Bracelet, 7 in. (18 cm)

- 5 g 8º seed beads, silver-lined matte dark gold luster
- 5 g 11º seed beads, transparent gold luster
- 5 g 11º seed beads, matte brown iris
- 5 g 11º seed beads, silver-lined matte gold luster
- 1 g 15º seed beads, transparent gold luster
- **61** 3 mm bicone crystals, crystal golden shadow
- **5** 4 mm bicone crystals, crystal golden shadow
- 14 mm rivoli crystal, crystal golden shadow
- **2** 4 mm spacer beads
- **3** 5 mm spacer beads
- toggle clasp
- **4** 4 mm jump rings
- **4** 2 mm crimp tubes
- **6** 1 mm crimp tubes
- **6** 4 mm crimp covers
- 12 in. (30 cm) gold beading wire, .014
- 12 in. antique brass beading wire, .018
- 12 in. beading wire, .014
- tool kit, p. 71

Note: All findings are gold-filled.

Techniques

Starting a new thread, p. 74
Securing thread, p. 75
Applying a crimp cover, p. 76
Folded crimps, p. 76
Opening and closing jump rings, p. 77

Earrings

1 Create a sunflower pendant following steps 1–8 of "Sunflower Pendant," except make the wire loops ½ in. (1.3 cm) to create smaller flower petals.

2 Attach an earring hook to the flower petal to complete the earrings.

3 Repeat steps 1 and 2 to make a second earring.

Materials

Earrings, 2 in. (5 cm)

- 5 g 8º seed beads, silver-lined matte dark gold luster
- 5 g 11º seed beads, transparent gold luster
- 5 g 11º seed beads, matte brown iris
- 5 g 11º seed beads, silver-lined matte gold luster
- 1 g 15º seed beads, transparent gold luster
- **10** 3 mm bicone crystals, crystal golden shadow
- **10** 4 mm bicone crystals, crystal golden shadow
- **2** 14 mm rivoli crystal, crystal golden shadow
- **4** 1 mm crimp tubes
- **4** 4 mm crimp covers
- **6** 4 mm spacer beads
- **4** 5 mm spacer beads
- pair of earring hooks
- 12 in. (30 cm) gold beading wire, .014
- 12 in. antique brass beading wire, .018
- tool kit, p. 71

Note: All findings are gold-filled.

Techniques

Starting a new thread, p. 74

Securing thread, p. 75

Folded crimps, p. 76

Applying a crimp cover, p. 76

Making simple loops, p. 77

Opening and closing jump rings, p. 77

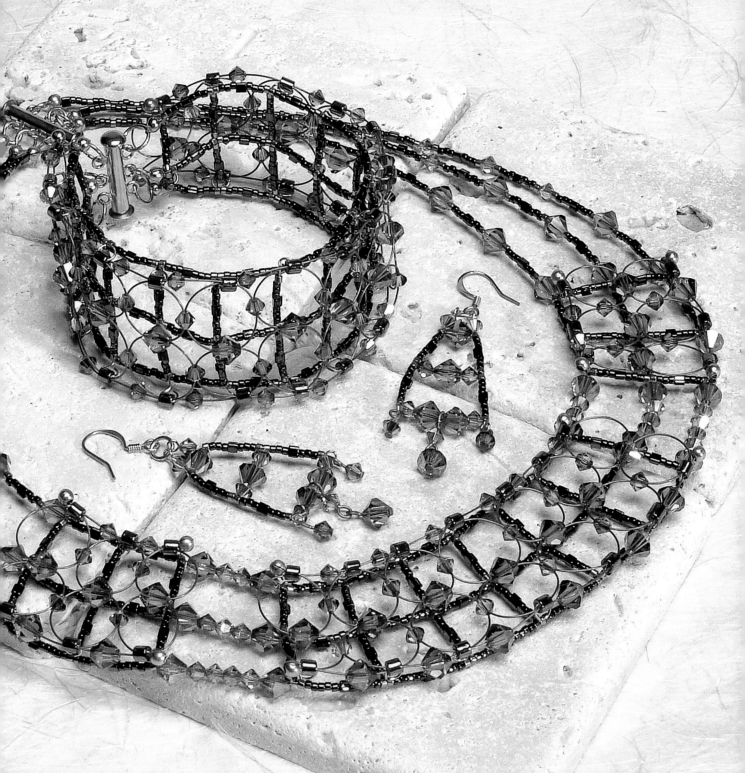

Body Language

Sometimes just a glance at the world around you opens up a realm of possibilities. For this piece, I was inspired by delicate lace that I saw at a friend's house, and I started playing with the idea of using layered beadwork with simple construction. I absolutely love this design because it's very minimalist, but you can't miss the sparkle of the crystals.

Skill level: Intermediate

Materials

Necklace, 18 in. (45 cm)

- 8 g 11º cylinder seed beads, metallic raspberry
- 5 g 11º cylinder seed beads, bright copper
- 5 g 11º triangle beads, metallic raspberry
- 5 g 8º cylinder seed beads, red gold luster
- **53** 6 mm bicone crystals, crystal copper
- **66** 4 mm bicone crystals, crystal copper
- 3-loop slide clasp
- **18** 1 mm crimp tubes
- **18** 4 mm crimp covers
- **6** 4 mm jump rings
- 1 yd. (.9 m) half-hard, 24-gauge, copper wire
- 10 ft. (3.0 m) beading wire, .014, bright copper color
- 2 yd. (1.8 m) beading wire, .012, silver color
- tool kit, p. 71

Note: All findings are copper.

Techniques

Starting a new thread, p. 74
Attaching a new thread, p. 74
Securing thread, p. 75
Flattened crimp, p. 76
Applying a crimp cover, p. 76
Making loops, p. 77
Opening and closing jump rings, p. 77

Necklace

Creating the Necklace Base

1 Cut three 24-in. (61 cm) strands of .012 silver-colored beading wire and place a Bead Stopper 3 in. (8 cm) left of the center on each strand.

2 On one strand, pick up a pattern of an 11º copper cylinder seed bead, three 11º metallic raspberry cylinder seed beads, an 11º triangle bead, three 11º metallic raspberry cylinders, and an 11º copper cylinder two times, and then pick up a 6 mm bicone, two 4 mm bicones, and a 6 mm bicone. Pick up the seed bead pattern again six more times, followed by the same pattern of bicones. Pick up two more sets of seed beads and place a Bead Stopper on the wire.

3 On the second strand, pick up the same pattern as in step 2, except add a 4 mm bicone so there are three 4 mm bicones between the two 6 mm bicones, and pick up four 11º metallic raspberry cylinders instead of three. Place a Bead Stopper after the crystals.

4 On the third strand, pick up the same pattern as step 1, except pick up four 4 mm bicones between the 6 mm bicones and pick up five 11º metallic raspberry cylinders in each seed bead set.

5 Cut a comfortable length of beading thread and go through the first and second copper cylinders (and all the beads between) of the first beaded strand.

6 Pick up an 11º copper cylinder, three 11º metallic raspberry cylinders, a triangle, three 11º metallic raspberry cylinders, and an 11º copper cylinder. Pass through (from right to left) the first and second 11º copper cylinders (and all the beads between) of the second strand (**figure 1**).

7 Pick up the same bead pattern as in step 6, and go through the first and second copper cylinders of the first strand again. Pass through the third and fourth 11º copper cylinders on the same strand and repeat step 6, except pass up through the previous set of beads before passing through the third and fourth 11º copper cylinders (**figure 2**).

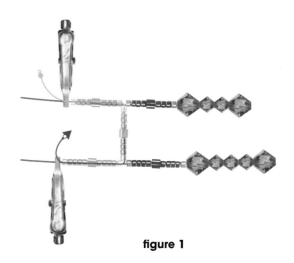

figure 1

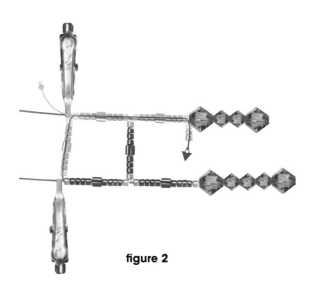

figure 2

"I make an effort to jot down something that inspires me every day. Even silly ideas can turn into brilliant designs."

8 Go through the bicones to the next set of seed beads, and repeat the stitching to complete the first section of the necklace base.

9 Repeat steps 5–7 to stitch the third beaded strand.

Creating the Eye Pins

1 Cut a 2-in. (5 cm) piece of half-hard wire and make a simple loop at one end. String an 8º cylinder on the loop.

2 Pass the wire through the vertical seed beads and make another simple loop (**figure 3**).

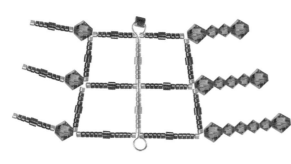

figure 3

3 String an 8º cylinder on the simple loop and use bentnose pliers to bend both heads of the simple loop straight up.

Weaving the Beading Wire

1 Cut a 6-in. (15 cm) piece of copper-colored beading wire. Crimp the end and apply a crimp cover.

2 Go clockwise through the first 8º cylinder, pick up a 4 mm bicone and a 6 mm bicone, and pass through the 8º cylinder again. Pick up a 4 mm bicone and go through the next 8º cylinder. Pick up a 4 mm bicone and a 6 mm bicone and go up through the first 4 mm bicone and through the 8º cylinder (**figure 4**). Repeat this step and place a Bead Stopper at the end of the wire.

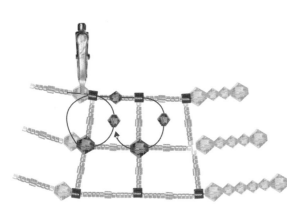

figure 4

3 Repeat steps 1 and 2 to weave through the bottom 8º cylinders. Remove the Bead Stopper from the copper beading wire, adjust the loops so they are even, and crimp the wire ends. Apply a crimp cover to finish the first panel.

4 Repeat steps 1–3 for the middle and right panels to complete the wire weaving.

Finish the Necklace

1 Remove the Bead Stopper from the first strand. Pick up a 6 mm bicone and the seed bead pattern from step 2 of "Creating the Necklace Base" seven times, except pick up a 6 mm bicone between each pattern of seed beads three times and pick up a 4 mm bicone three times. The necklace strand should end with a seed bead pattern. Crimp the end to a jump ring and apply a crimp cover.

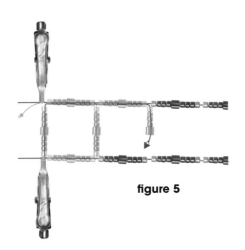

figure 5

2 Repeat step 1 for the remaining two strands, except pick up the seed bead pattern nine times on the middle strand, with three 6 mm bicones, and 11 seed bead patterns, with two 6 mm bicones, on the last strand.

3 Repeat steps 1 and 2 for the other side. Attach the jump rings to the bar clasp to complete the necklace design.

Bracelet

1 Cut three 12-in. (30 cm) strands of .012 silver-colored beading wire and place a Bead Stopper at the end of each strand.

2 On each strand, pick up a pattern of: an 11º copper cylinder bead, three 11º metallic raspberry cylinder beads, an 11º triangle bead, three 11º metallic raspberry cylinders, and an 11º copper cylinder 14 times, and place another Bead Stopper at the end.

3 Cut a comfortable length of beading thread and go through the first 11º copper cylinder and the second 11º copper cylinder of the first beaded strand. Pick up a set of seed beads as in step 1, and pass from right to left through the second 11º copper cylinder bead through the first 11º cylinder bead of the second beaded strand.

4 Pick up a set of seed beads as in step 1, and pass through the second 11º copper cylinder of the first beaded strand again. Pass through the third and fourth cylinder, and repeat the stitching method from step 3 for the rest of this row and the next row as well to create a grid (**figure 5**). Attach thread as needed. Secure the threads when you have completed the bracelet base.

5 Remove the Bead Stoppers and create a folded crimp, attaching a 4 mm jump ring to the middle wire and a 6 mm jump ring to the outer two wires. Attach the jump rings to the clasp.

6 Create the beaded eye pins and insert them into the grid following steps 1–3 of "Creating the Eye Pins."

7 Weave the beading wire through the beaded eye pins following steps 1–3 of "Weaving the Beading Wire."

Materials
Bracelet, 7 in. (18 cm)
- 5 g 11º cylinder seed beads, metallic raspberry
- 4 g 11º cylinder seed beads, bright copper
- 4 g 11º triangle beads, metallic raspberry
- 4 g 8º cylinder seed beads, red gold luster
- **15** 6 mm bicone crystals, crystal copper
- **56** 4 mm bicone crystals, crystal copper
- 3-loop slide clasp
- **10** 1 mm crimp tubes
- **10** 4 mm crimp covers
- **2** 4 mm jump rings
- **4** 6 mm jump rings
- 24 in. (61 cm) half-hard, 24-gauge copper wire
- 2 yd. (1.8 m) beading wire, .014, bright copper color
- 1 yd. (.9 m) beading wire, .012, silver color
- tool kit, p. 71

Note: All findings are sterling silver.

Techniques
Starting a new thread, p. 74
Attaching a new thread, p. 74
Securing thread, p. 75
Folded crimp, p. 75
Flattened crimp, p. 76
Applying a crimp cover, p. 76
Opening and closing jump rings, p. 77

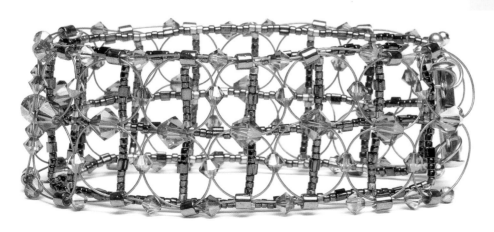

Earrings

Materials

Earrings, 2 in. (5 cm)

- 1 g 11º cylinder seed beads, metallic raspberry
- 1 g 11º cylinder beads, bright copper
- 1 g 11º triangle beads, metallic raspberry
- **10** 6 mm bicone crystals, crystal copper
- **18** 4 mm bicone crystals, crystal copper
- pair of earring hooks
- **2** 4 mm jump rings
- 8 in. (20 cm) half-hard 24-gauge copper wire
- **6** 1-in. (2 cm) head pins
- tool kit, p. 71

Techniques

Starting a new thread, p. 74
Securing thread, p. 75
Making loops, p. 77
Opening and closing jump rings, p. 77

1 With the half-hard copper wire, create three dangles with a simple loop on one end of each. Create two dangles using a 4 mm bicone, and one dangle using a 6 mm bicone. Create another dangle using a 4 mm bicone with a simple loop on both sides of the bead. Attach that dangle to the 6 mm bicone dangle.

2 Cut a comfortable length of beading thread and pick up the following set of beads: An 11º copper cylinder bead, three 11º metallic raspberry cylinder beads, an 11º triangle bead, three 11º metallic raspberry cylinders, and an 11º copper cylinder. Then pick up a 4 mm bicone, a 6 mm bicone, and a 4 mm bicone. Repeat the first set of beads. Pick up a 4 mm bicone, a 6 mm bicone, the 6 mm bicone dangle, a 6 mm bicone, and a 4 mm bicone.

3 Pass up through the first set of seed beads to form a loop. Pass through the three bicones and pick up the same set of seed beads as before, a 6 mm crystal, and another set of seed beads.

4 Pass through the three bicones to create another loop and stitch through the beads to meet the other end of the thread (**figure 6**). Secure the threads.

5 Cut 2 in. (5 cm) of half-hard wire and create a simple loop at one end. Pass the wire through the seed beads of both loops, pick up a 4 mm bicone, and make another simple loop at the top. Repeat this step for the other side of the earring.

6 Attach the jump ring to both simple loops and attach the dangles to the bottom simple loops.

7 Attach an earring hook to the jump ring.

8 Repeat steps 1–7 to make a second earring.

figure 6

Cosmic

Cosmic was one of those pieces that I started with one idea and went completely in the opposite direction. That's how some things go, I suppose. Initially I was inspired by graffiti art, but as the construction developed, I ended up mixing several other techniques together to create this design. Constructing this piece was quite effortless and lots of fun. I hope you have as much fun making and wearing your own version!

Skill level: Intermediate/advanced

Materials
Necklace, 28 in. (71 cm)

- **40 g** 4 mm cube beads, matte metallic gold rainbow
- **24** 3 mm triangle beads, matte metallic gold rainbow
- **5 g** 15º seed beads, transparent violet luster
- **23** 6 mm round spacer beads, antique copper
- **17** 4 mm round spacer beads, antique copper
- **6** 6 mm bicone crystals in each of **3** colors: light amethyst, amethyst, and tanzanite
- **10** 4 mm bicone crystals in each of **3** colors: light amethyst, amethyst, and tanzanite
- **81** 3 mm bicone crystals in each of **3** colors: light amethyst, amethyst, and tanzanite
- S-hook clasp
- **24** 4 mm jump rings
- **17** 2 mm crimp tubes
- **17** 4 mm crimp covers
- 2 yd. (1.8 m) beading wire, .014, copper color
- tool kit, p. 71

Note: All findings are antique copper.

Techniques
Starting a new thread, p. 74
Attaching a new thread, p. 74
Securing thread, p. 75
Folded crimp, p. 76
Applying a crimp cover, p. 76
Opening and closing jump rings, p. 77

Necklace

Crystal Triangles

1 Cut a comfortable length of beading thread and string two 4 mm cube beads. Pass up through the first cube bead and down through the second cube bead and pick up another cube bead. Pass down through the second cube bead and up through the new cube bead. Repeat this stitch until five cube beads are stitched together.

2 Stitch another cube bead and position it next to the last cube bead as shown. Stitch three more cube beads together (**figure 1**).

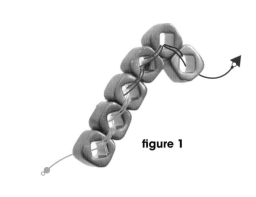

figure 1

3 Stitch a 3 mm triangle bead and position it inside the stitched right angle made by the cube beads. Go through the next cube bead and pick up a new cube bead so that it sits next to the triangle bead. With the thread exiting the new cube bead, stitch another cube bead onto it. Go through the new cube bead and stitch into the cube bead of the sewn right angle (**figure 2**). Continue to stitch the remaining cube beads and end the crystal triangle with a triangle bead stitched to the last cube bead. Secure the threads to finish the grid.

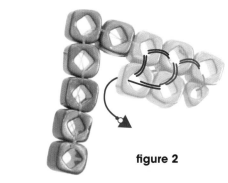

figure 2

4 Start a new thread and go up through a cube bead. Pick up a 3 mm bicone of any color and a 15º seed bead and pass down through the 3 mm bicone and cube bead. Go up through the next cube bead (**figure 3**) and repeat this stitch, picking up 3 mm bicones of random color, but skip stitching a bicone in the corner cube bead. Secure the loose threads to finish.

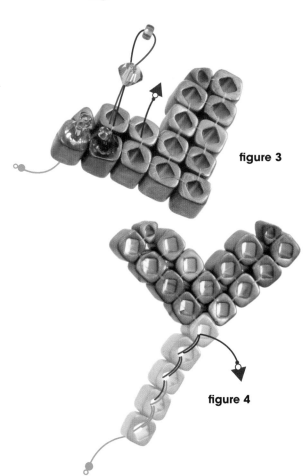

figure 3

Small Crystal Argyles

1 Following steps 1–3 of "Crystal Triangles," create a crystal triangle, but do not add the 3 mm bicones.

2 Start a new thread and stitch four cube beads together.

3 Go through the corner cube bead of the crystal triangle component and stitch it to the line of cube beads. The thread should exit the corner cube bead (**figure 4**). Stitch four cube beads together. Stitch a triangle bead to the last cube bead and position it inside of the right angle made by the cube beads. Continue stitching the remaining cube beads to the inner part of the right angle made by the cube beads. Secure the loose threads to complete the grid.

figure 4

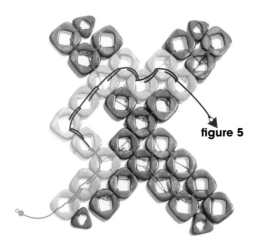

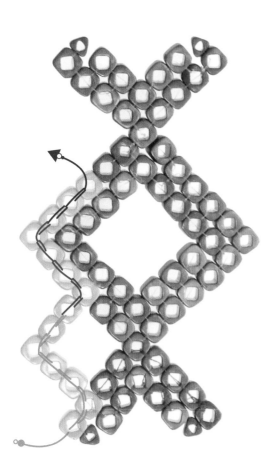

figure 5

④ To stitch the sides of the small crystal argyle, start a new thread and go through the outer left third cube bead from the bottom part of the small crystal argyle and stitch one cube bead to that cube bead. Stitch two more cube beads together and position the last cube bead to the right to create a corner with the cube beads. Go through that cube bead to the third upper left cube bead and pass through the cube beads of the small crystal argyle until the thread exits the third upper right cube bead (**figure 5**). Stitch three cube beads together and position the last cube bead to the left and stitch it to the third bottom left cube bead.

⑤ Use the remaining thread to stitch 3 mm bicones into each cube bead. Secure the threads. Create four small crystal argyles and set them aside.

Large Crystal Argyle
① Create two crystal triangles without stitching the 3 mm bicones (follow steps 1–3 of "Crystal Triangles"). Start with a comfortable length of thread, go through one of the crystal triangles, and go up through the corner cube bead.

② Stitch seven cube beads together. Shift the last cube bead to the right to create a right angle and stitch four more cube beads together. Stitch the corner cube bead of the other crystal triangle to the stitched cubes. The thread should exit the corner cube bead.

③ Continue stitching the cube beads for the other side to complete the square. Use the remaining thread to stitch cube beads to the inside of the beaded square. Secure the loose threads.

④ Start a new thread, go up through the left middle cube bead of the crystal triangle, and stitch four cube beads together. Shift the last cube bead to the right and stitch two more cube beads together. Stitch the last cube bead to the fourth left cube bead of the beaded square and pass through the beaded square to reach the upper middle cube bead of the beaded square (**figure 6**). Stitch the remaining right angles for both sides. Secure the loose threads.

⑤ Start a new thread; stitch the 3 mm bicones into the cube beads. Secure the loose threads after stitching the last bicone.

figure 6

Illusion Links

1 Cut 12 in. (30 cm) of beading wire and place a Bead Stopper 1 in. (2.5 cm) from the end.

2 Choosing the crystal colors randomly, string a 6 mm copper spacer, a 4 mm bicone, a 4 mm copper spacer, a 6 mm copper spacer, a 4 mm bicone and a 6 mm bicone.

3 Pass the wire through the 6 mm copper spacer to create a loop and then go through the 4 mm copper spacer, skipping the 4 mm bicone. Go through the next 6 mm copper spacer and the 6 mm bicone, and then go through the first 6 mm copper spacer again **(figure 7)**. Go through the 4 mm bicone and the second 6 mm copper spacer.

4 Go through the 4 mm bicone and string a crimp. Remove the Bead Stopper and thread it into the crimp so the wires cross each other. Leave a ½-in. (1.3 cm) length on each wire end and make a folded crimp. Trim the excess wire close to the crimp and apply a crimp cover to finish the beaded ring.

5 Create three illusion links and set them aside.

Illusion Chain

1 Create one illusion chain link following steps 1–4 of "Illusion Links."

2 Create a second illusion chain, but instead of stringing a second 6 mm spacer, pass the wire through the 6 mm copper spacer of the previous ring so that the rings connect.

3 Create two illusion chains with five links and another illusion chain with four links connected as in step 2.

Assemble the Necklace

1 Attach an illusion chain link to the large crystal argyle and the small crystal argyle with jump rings. The 6 mm copper spacer should be between the triangle beads.

2 Connect the remaining illusion chains and argyles the same way, with the four-link chain on the upper left section of the necklace and the five-link chain on the bottom middle section and the top right section of the necklace.

3 Attach the crystal triangles created earlier to the ends of the chains.

4 Attach S-hook jump rings to both of the empty cube beads of the crystal triangles to finish the necklace.

figure 7

Materials

Bracelet, 8 in. (20 cm)

- 25 g 4 mm cube beads, matte metallic gold rainbow
- **20** 3 mm triangle beads, matte metallic gold rainbow
- 2–3 g 15º seed beads, transparent violet luster
- **6** 6 mm round spacer beads, antique copper
- **3** 4 mm round spacer beads, antique copper
- **2** 6 mm bicone crystals in each of **3** colors: light amethyst, amethyst, and tanzanite
- **2** 4 mm bicone crystals in each of **3** colors: light amethyst, amethyst, and tanzanite
- **42** 3 mm bicone crystals in each of **3** colors: light amethyst, amethyst, and tanzanite
- S-hook clasp
- **16** 4 mm jump rings
- **4** 2 mm crimp tubes
- **4** 4 mm crimp covers
- 5 ft. (1.5 m) beading wire, .014, copper color
- tool kit, p. 71

Note: All findings are antique copper.

Techniques

Starting a new thread, p. 74
Attaching a new thread, p. 74
Securing thread, p. 75
Folded crimp, p. 76
Applying a crimp cover, p. 76
Opening and closing jump rings, p. 77

Bracelet

1 Create two crystal triangles following steps 1–4 of "Crystal Triangles."

2 Create three small crystal argyles following steps 1–5 of "Small Crystal Argyles."

3 Create four ¾-in. (2 cm) illusion links following steps 1–4 of "Illusion Links."

4 Attach an illusion chain link between each small crystal argyle and the two crystal triangles by attaching jump rings to the triangle beads and then onto the illusion link, with the 6 mm spacer placed between the triangle beads.

5 To finish the bracelet, attach an S-hook jump ring to each empty cube bead on the beaded crystal triangles.

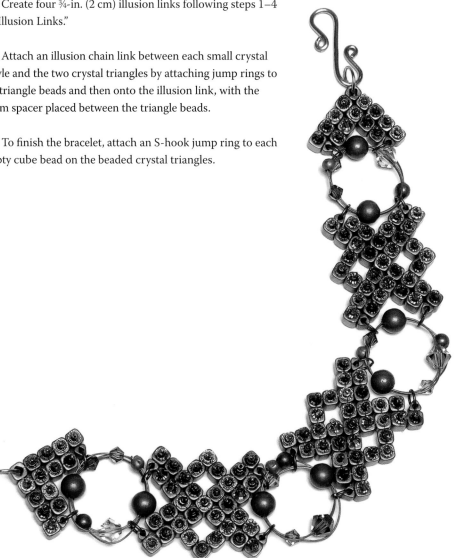

Materials

Earrings, 1½ in. (4 cm)

- 10 g 4 mm cube beads, matte metallic gold rainbow
- **4** 3 mm triangle beads, matte metallic gold rainbow
- 1–2 g 15º seed beads, transparent violet luster
- **2** 6 mm round spacer beads, antique copper
- **2** 4 mm round spacer beads, antique copper
- **2** 6 mm bicone crystals in your choice of **3** colors: light amethyst, amethyst, or tanzanite
- **4** 4 mm bicone crystals in your choice of **3** colors: light amethyst, amethyst, or tanzanite
- **28** 3 mm bicone crystals in your choice of **3** colors: light amethyst, amethyst, or tanzanite
- pair of earring hooks
- **4** 4 mm jump rings
- **2** 6 mm jump rings
- **2** 2 mm crimp tubes
- **2** 4 mm crimp covers
- 24 in. (61 cm) beading wire, .014, copper color
- tool kit, p. 71

Note: All findings are antique copper.

Techniques

Starting a new thread, p. 74
Securing thread, p. 75
Folded crimp, p. 76
Applying a crimp cover, p. 76
Opening and closing jump rings, p. 77

Earrings

1 Create two beaded crystal triangles following steps 1–4 of "Crystal Triangles," but stitch a 3 mm bicone in the colors of your choice in all the cube beads.

2 Create two ¾-in. (2 cm) illusion chain links following steps 1–4 of "Illusion Links," but replace one of the 6 mm spacers with a 4 mm spacer.

3 Attach an illusion link between the crystal triangle by attaching jump rings to the triangle beads and then to the illusion link, with the 6 mm spacer placed between the triangle beads. Attach a 6 mm jump ring to the 4 mm spacer and an earring hook onto the jump ring to complete the earring.

4 Repeat steps 1–3 to make a second earring.

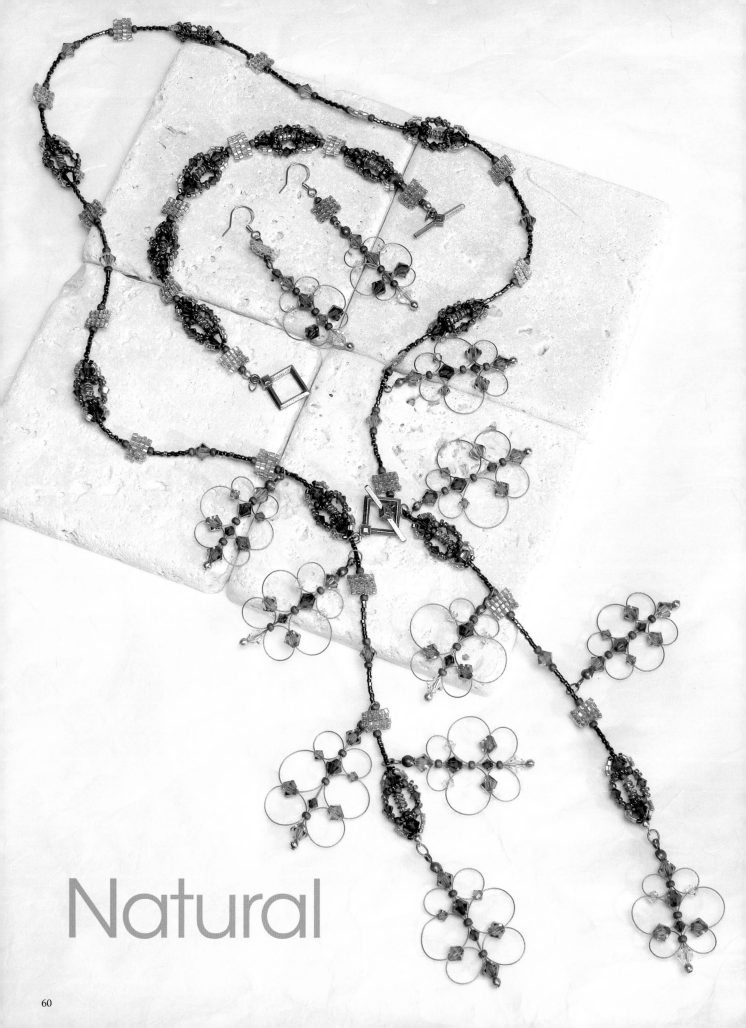

Natural

For Natural, I was inspired by leaf veins and reinterpreted them using beading wire and crystals to give the pendants an airy feel. The thing I love about this design is that it is quick and easy to put together, and it's perfect for just about any occasion. From the workplace to drinks at night, this piece is effortless to wear again and again.

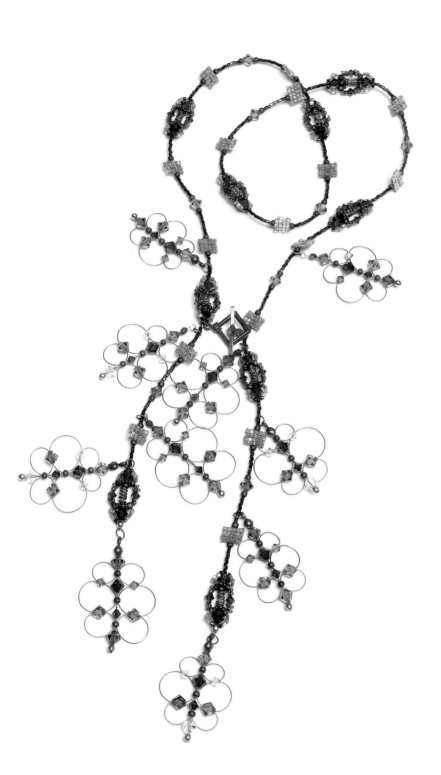

Materials

Necklace, 38 in. (97 cm)

- 5 g 11º seed beads, green luster
- 5 g 8º seed beads, matte olive green
- 5 g 2 mm cube beads, lime-lined yellow luster
- 3 g 11º cylinder beads, metallic green iris
- **28** 6 mm bicone crystals, tourmaline
- **28** 4 mm bicone crystals, tourmaline
- **41** 6 mm bicone crystals, olivine
- **12** 4 mm bicone crystals, olivine
- **4** 6 mm bicone crystals, jonquil
- **8** 4 mm bicone crystals, jonquil
- toggle clasp
- **12** 4 mm jump rings
- **10** clamshells
- **12** 2 mm crimp tubes
- **12** 4 mm crimp covers
- 10 1-in. (2.5 cm) head pins
- 10 ft. (3 m) beading wire, .014, copper color
- 42 in. (1.07 cm) beading wire, .014, silver color
- tool kit, p. 71

Note: All findings are antique copper.

Techniques

Starting a new thread, p. 74
Attaching a new thread, p. 74
Securing thread, p. 75
Flattened crimp, p. 76
Applying a crimp cover, p. 76
Attaching a clamshell, p. 76
Opening and closing jump rings, p. 77

figure 1

figure 2

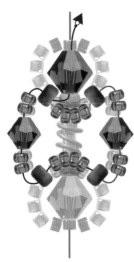

figure 3

Necklace

Necklace Rope

① Place a Bead Stopper at one end of the silver-colored beading wire.

② String the following pattern eight times: 6 mm tourmaline bicone, 8º seed bead, four 2 mm cube beads (see note), 8º, 6 mm tourmaline bicone, 10 11º cylinder beads, an 8º, four cube beads, 8º, 10 11º cylinders, 8º, 6 mm olivine bicone, 8º, 10 11º cylinders, 8º, four cube beads, 8º, and 10 11º cylinders. End the pattern with a 6 mm tourmaline bicone, an 8º, four cube beads (see note), an 8º, and a 6 mm tourmaline bicone.

NOTE The cube beads between the 6 mm tourmaline bicones have a wire coil around them. Cut the head off a head pin. Coil the wire around a cylinder that has a 2 mm diameter, such as an ice pick or a wooden skewer, and spread the coils to fill up the space of the cube beads. Trim the ends of the wire and string the wire over the cube beads.

③ Cut a comfortable length of beading thread. Pass up through the first 6 mm tourmaline bicone and pick up an 8º, three cube beads, and a cylinder. Pass up through the 6 mm tourmaline bicone again and pick up the same bead pattern as before. Pass up through the 6 mm tourmaline bicone again and then pass through all the beads until you reach the second 6 mm tourmaline bicone. Pick up a cylinder, three cube beads, and an 8º. Pass up through the 6 mm tourmaline crystal, pick up another set of a cylinder, three cube beads, and an 8º, and pass up through the 6 mm tourmaline bicone again (**figure 1**).

④ Pass through the cylinder, three cube beads, and the 8º on the right side, and pick up four 11º seed beads. Pass through the left 8º and pick up two 11ºs, a 4 mm tourmaline bicone, and two 11ºs. Pass through the bottom left 8º, pick up four 11ºs, and pass through the bottom right 8º (**figure 2**). Pick up the same pattern of 11ºs and 4 mm bicone, and pass through the top right 8º. Turn the stitched piece over. Pick up four 11ºs and pass through the top right 8º. Pick up two 11ºs and pass down through the 4 mm and pick up two 11ºs. Pass through the bottom right 8º and pick up four 11ºs. Pass through the left 8º and pick up two 11ºs. Pass up through the 4 mm bicone, pick up two 11ºs, and pass through the 8º and then up through the 6 mm bicone (**figure 3**).

⑤ Pass through the 10 cylinders, the 8º, and four cube beads of the strung beads.

⑥ Pick up two cube beads and pass up through the last two previous cube beads and then down through the new cube beads. Pick up two cube beads (**figure 4**) and pass up through the bottom two cube beads of the strung beads, and down through the new cube beads. Pick up two cube beads (**figure 5),** and pass down through the two cubes of the previous stitch. Pass up through the two new cubes and pick up two more cubes. Pass down through the top two cubes of the previous row. Pass through down through the bottom two cubes of the strung beads, pick up two cubes **(figure 6),** and repeat the stitching to create two rows. Then stitch through the strung cube beads to continue the rope.

7 Repeat steps 4–6 to stitch the beaded ovals and the beaded squares for the remainder of the necklace design. Secure any loose threads.

8 Remove the Bead Stoppers and crimp the ends to a jump ring. Apply a crimp cover and set this piece aside.

Woven Pendants

1 Cut two 6-in. (15 cm) strands of copper-colored beading wire and hold them so the ends are even. Pick up a crimp tube and crimp both wires together at the end. Apply a crimp cover. On both wires, pick up a 6 mm olivine bicone and an 8º.

2 String a 6 mm olivine bicone on each wire and pass both wires up through the 8º to form loops. Adjust both loops to be about 8 mm.

NOTE It's a good idea to keep track of which wire created the right loop and which created the left loop, and to use the same wires consistently for their respective sides. This will make adjusting the loops easier and less confusing.

3 Pick up a 4 mm tourmaline bicone and an 8º on both wires **(figure 7).** String a 4 mm olivine bicone on each wire, pass each wire through the 6 mm olivine bicone of the previous loops, and then pass both wires up through the 8º to form the second set of loops. Adjust the loops so they are bigger than the first set of loops.

4 Pick up a 6 mm tourmaline bicone and an 8º on both wires. Pass each wire through the 4 mm olivine bicone of the previous set of loops, and then pass both wires up through the 8º. Adjust these loops to be smaller than the first set of loops.

5 Pick up a 6 mm olivine bicone **(figure 8).** Crimp both ends, and attach a clamshell to both wires with a jump ring attached to the clamshell hook to create a woven pendant.

6 Create nine more woven pendants.

NOTE You can get creative and customize the weave by adjusting the tension to create bigger or smaller loops to alter the weave pattern or by changing the colors of the crystals. You can make the pendants all the same or very different, depending on your taste.

Assembling the Necklace

1 Attach five woven pendants, spaced 1 in. (2.5 cm) apart, on each side of the necklace rope.

2 Attach the clasp just below the top woven pendant to complete the necklace.

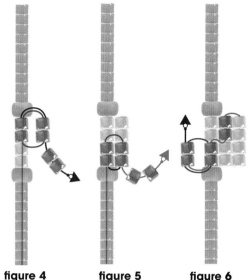

figure 4   **figure 5**   **figure 6**

figure 7

figure 8

Bracelet

1 Place a Bead Stopper at the end of the silver-colored beading wire.

2 String the following pattern five times: 8º seed bead, four cube beads, 8º cylinder bead, 6 mm tourmaline bicone, 8º, four cube beads (see note), 8º, 6 mm tourmaline bicone, and 11º cylinder. End the pattern with an 8º, four cube beads, and an 8º.

NOTE The cube beads between the 6 mm tourmaline bicones have a wire coil around them. Take your head pin and cut the head off. Coil the wire around a cylinder that has a 2 mm diameter, such as an ice pick or a wooden skewer, and spread the coils to fill up the space of the cube beads. Trim the ends of the wire and string over the cube beads.

3 Cut a comfortable length of beading thread and follow steps 3–7, omitting step 5, of "Necklace Rope." Start as in step 6, and then work as in step 3 after you reach the first 6 mm tourmaline bicone.

4 Secure any loose threads and crimp the ends to a jump ring. Apply a crimp cover and attach the clasp to finish the bracelet.

Materials

Bracelet, 8½ in. (21.6 cm)

- 5 g 11º seed beads, green luster
- 5 g 8º seed beads, matte olive green
- 5 g 2 mm cube beads, lime lined yellow luster
- 2 g 11º cylinder beads, metallic green iris
- **10** 6 mm bicone crystals, tourmaline
- **10** 4 mm bicone crystals, tourmaline
- toggle clasp
- **2** 4 mm jump rings
- **2** 2 mm crimp tubes
- **2** 4 mm crimp covers
- **5** 1-in. (2.5 cm) head pins
- 12 in. (30 cm) beading wire, .014, silver color
- tool kit, p. 71

Note: All findings are antique copper.

Techniques

Starting a new thread, p. 74
Attaching a new thread, p. 74
Securing thread, p. 75
Folded crimp, p. 76
Applying a crimp cover, p. 76
Opening and closing jump rings, p. 77

Earrings

1. Create a small woven pendant following steps 1–5 of "Woven Pendant." Pull each wire so that the outer loops are about 6 mm and the middle loop is about 10 mm before adding a crimp and attaching a clamshell, and substitute the crystal colors as indicated in the diagram (**figure 9**).

2. Cut a comfortable length of beading thread and place a Bead Stopper at one end. Pick up four 2 mm cube beads, and then follow step 6 of "Necklace Rope" to create the beaded square. Secure the loose threads.

3. On an eye pin, pick up an 8º seed bead, a beaded square, and an 8º, and make a simple loop.

4. Attach the woven pendant to one end of the eye pin. Attach an earring hook to the simple loop at the other end to finish the earring.

5. Repeat steps 1–4 to make a second earring.

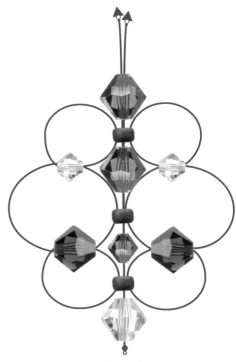

figure 9

Materials

Earrings, 2½ in. (6 cm)

- **10** 8º seed beads, matte olive green
- **40** 2 mm cube beads, lime-lined yellow luster
- **4** 6 mm bicone crystals, tourmaline
- **4** 6 mm bicone crystals, olivine
- **2** 6 mm bicone crystals, jonquil
- **2** 4 mm bicone crystals, olivine
- **4** 4 mm bicone crystals, jonquil
- pair of earring hooks
- **2** clamshells
- **2** 2 mm crimp tubes
- **2** 4 mm crimp covers
- **2** 2-in. (5 cm) eye pins
- 24 in. (61 cm) beading wire, .014, copper color
- tool kit, p. 71

Note: All findings are antique copper.

Techniques

Starting a new thread, p. 74
Securing thread, p. 75
Folded crimp, p. 76
Attaching a clamshell, p. 76
Applying a crimp cover, p. 76
Making loops, p. 77
Opening and closing jump rings, p. 77

Behind the Beads

Designing a Piece

I've been able to develop a specific designing method that works perfectly for me, and now I have the wonderful opportunity to share this with you. I hope that you will feel encouraged and inspired to try designing yourself. I've organized this design process into five stages that are broken down according to the development of a jewelry design.

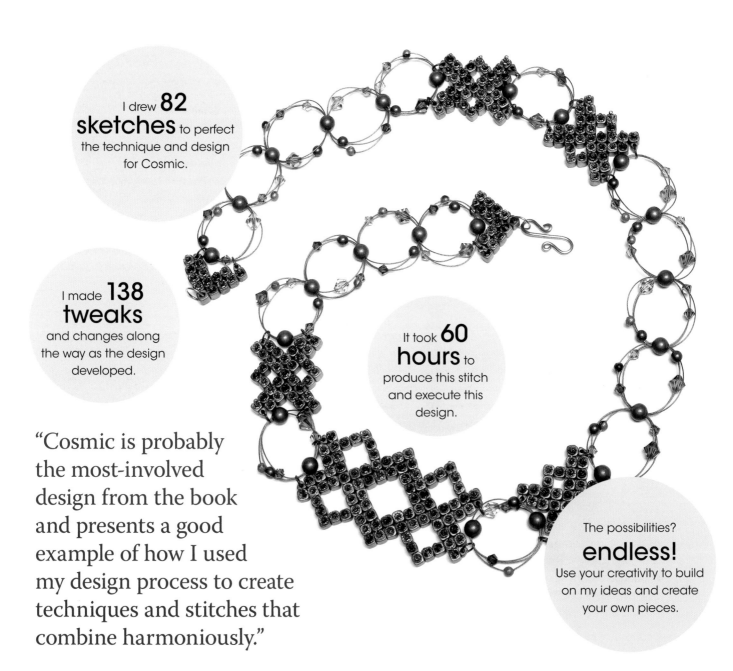

I drew **82 sketches** to perfect the technique and design for Cosmic.

I made **138 tweaks** and changes along the way as the design developed.

It took **60 hours** to produce this stitch and execute this design.

The possibilities? **endless!** Use your creativity to build on my ideas and create your own pieces.

"Cosmic is probably the most-involved design from the book and presents a good example of how I used my design process to create techniques and stitches that combine harmoniously."

1 Gathering Ideas *Thinking outside the box*

Typically, I like to gather my ideas by closely examining my materials or beads. Rather than seeing a material for what it literally is, I try to think of other possibilities or what else I can do with it. You can do this too. For example, pick up any random jewelry component or unusual bead, and begin to describe it out loud as though it was an alien artifact and you were telling your friend about it. Try turning it upside down, at an angle, or backward, and look for points of interest that could be useful for creating a nice focal piece or bridging other jewelry components together. Anything, whether it's used for jewelry or not, is capable of becoming a hundred different things—but only if you keep an open mind and look at it outside its normal use.

2 Sketching *Ideas make better sense on paper*

I like to use basic shapes, lines, and notations with arrows when I sketch my ideas. I try not to get too detailed when I'm doodling because if I become committed to an idea, my brain stops storming and I instantly become blocked with that one idea. This process is about constantly letting ideas flow onto paper before deciding which one works the best. My sketchbook not only includes drawings, but also photos, color palletes, and any other tidbits that I can refer to when I need to draw inspiration.

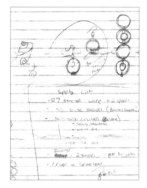

3 Demoing *It never hurts to give it a try*

Between sketches, I may come across a cool idea or stitch that I just have to try. I call this process "demoing," which means creating a small swatch of that particular sketch or technique idea, using spare beads, wire, or thread. By demonstrating the sketch or technique, I can figure out if it's going to work and be easy for someone else to replicate. This stage of the process is probably the longest, because I spend a good amount of time tweaking and perfecting the technique before moving forward.

4 Developing the Design *If it works, then make it so*

Once I've tested a new stitch or technique to see if it works, I develop a detailed sketch of the design and plan to make a demo swatch. With an intricate sketch, I can configure the beaded components and play with the connections. I usually run into many problems, but this step is important before making the actual design because I can resolve problems and come up with a clear plan for execution.

5 Production *A stickler for details*

I begin to work on the actual creation of the design after all the components are arranged and the techniques have been worked out. I also choose a color pallete by going through my seed beads and marking on the sketch where I would like to use certain beads, then pick the proper thread and wires to construct the design. All the small details, such as trimming excess thread, making sure wires don't stick out, and having clean stitch work, should be immaculate.

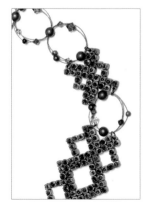

My work process is not as rigid as this breakdown seems because I have my share of happy accidents and screw-ups. The brilliant part of this process is how much I am able to draw inspiration for new ideas and execute them easily—it goes much faster than starting without any sort of plan. I hope you can take my work process as inspiration and try designing a piece yourself!

Materials & Techniques

Materials

This section lists the materials used for making the projects in this book. All of the materials can be found in any craft store, local bead store, or online bead supplier.

Beads

With so many choices available, it can be tough to choose the perfect beads for a design. This guide describes the beads I used to help make your selection process easier. There are so many types and styles of beads available, you're sure to find something in the right color and size to make the perfect piece of fabulous jewelry.

Crystal Beads

A crystal bead is made of glass and has a high content of lead oxide. The lead-infused glass causes light to refract at a high level and gives crystal its amazing brilliance. When purchasing crystal, make sure to carefully examine the facets to see if they are even and precise. Any scratches, cuts, or abrasions in the crystal bead may cut the beading thread or weaken the beading wire when constructing the design. The projects in this book use crystals made by Swarovski, because they are well known for their brilliant cut, color selection, and shape variety.

Rivoli Crystals

A rivoli crystal is a small crystal stone, made similarly to the crystal beads, and it's faceted to a point on the front and back. The back of the stone is foiled to enhance the appearance and shine of the front.

Glass Pearls

These pearls have a glass bead core that is layered with several coatings of paint. The brand of the glass pearl determines the quality and how it holds up to wear and abrasion so make sure to ask where they came from before purchasing. You can also check to see if the paint is chipping off, in which case you should avoid buying that strand.

Seed Beads

These tiny glass beads truly represent their name, because they are miniscule in size but absolutely a blast to work with. Seed beads are measured in a unit called an aught, represented by the symbol $^{\circ}$. As the size of the seed bead increases, the aught number decreases. The designs in this book use Japanese seed beads because they are uniform, have a wide bead hole, and come in a great variety of colors. You can substitute Czech seed beads, but the resulting design will be more organic and less even.

Cylinder Beads

Cylinder beads are short, tube-shaped beads with a large open hole and a thin wall. These Japanese beads are uniform in shape and size, and are available in most bead stores. Like seed beads, cylinders come in a variety of sizes and colors.

Cube Beads

Cube beads are square beads with a wide hole through the middle. Like seed beads, the size of cube beads is measured in aughts, and they comes in many colors. The mass of each cube bead results in a sturdy beaded foundation when stitched together. The large hole is great if you need to stitch through a bead many times.

Triangle Beads

Triangle beads are similar to cube beads, except they have three facets instead of four. These beads are perfect for adding a subtle texture or a pop of color to the beadwork. When shopping for triangles, make sure to note whether the triangle has sharp or soft edges. The projects in this book use both, but you may have a preference.

Bugle Beads

Similar to cylinder beads, bugle beads are cylinder-shaped beads, except they are elongated to form a thin tube. Bugle beads are great for speeding up tedious stitching work and creating a smooth texture when woven together. When shopping for bugle beads, take note of the ends of the beads. Sometimes the edges are worn and could potentially break your thread. Good-quality bugle beads are precision cut and should not have shattered ends.

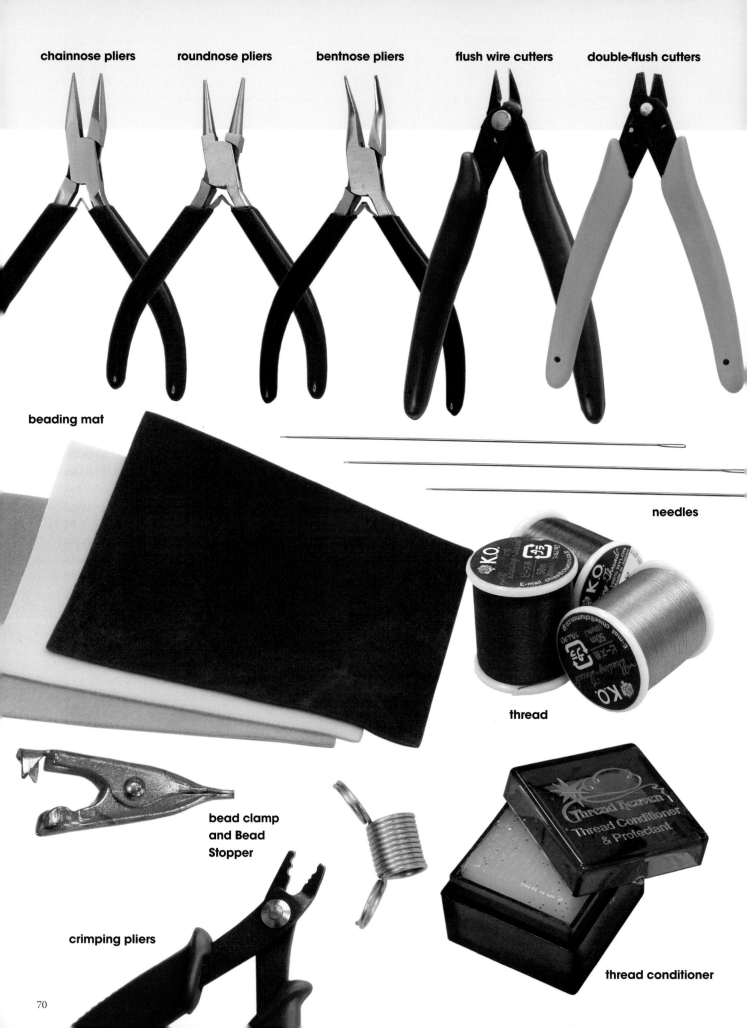

chainnose pliers

roundnose pliers

bentnose pliers

flush wire cutters

double-flush cutters

beading mat

needles

thread

bead clamp
and Bead
Stopper

crimping pliers

thread conditioner

scissors

Tool Kit

Having the correct tools will make beading easier and efficient. Trust me—I speak from experience! It took me a while to discover which tools are the most useful and easy to use, and then I finally invested in a really good set. Listed below are the basic tools. Be sure you have all of these in your tool kit to complete the projects in this book.

Chainnose Pliers

Chainnose pliers have a flat jaw that tapers to a narrow point at the tip. These pliers are great for opening and closing jump rings, pulling beading wire through tight spaces, and picking up small beads and components. Try to find a pair that have a very narrow tip because they are more versatile to use.

Roundnose Pliers

Roundnose pliers have a conical jaws that taper to a narrow tip. These pliers are used for creating simple loops. The size of the loop is determined by the placement of the metal wire within the pliers. If you want consistent loops, try using a marker to mark the spot on the pliers' nose where you want to form the loop. This way, all your loops will be the same size.

Bentnose Pliers

Bentnose pliers are similar to chainnose pliers, except they have a 45-degree bend in the midsection of the pliers, and the elongated tip comes to a very narrow point. Use these pliers for opening and closing jump rings, pushing the beading wire through small beads, and picking up small components.

Flush Wire Cutters

It's very important to distinguish this pair from your normal metal wire cutters. Flush cutters have tapered blades that come to a sharp point, and I use them exclusively to cut thread or beading wire only. If you start cutting metal wire with this pair, it will quickly wear out the blades and soon it won't be able to cut anything. So I recommend using these just for cutting thread or beading wire.

Double-flush Cutters

Double-flush cutters have blunt blades to create a blunt cut when cutting metal wire. The blunt cut is helpful for gripping the wire easily with your pliers and also creates a seamless appearance for simple loops.

Crimping Pliers

Crimping pliers are used to secure the crimp tubes to beading wire. The crimp pliers have two notches, or compartments, within the pliers for creating a folded crimp. These pliers are also useful for applying crimp covers.

Scissors

A small pair of sharp scissors dedicated to trimming beading thread is a great tool to have in your kit.

Needles

My favorite needle to use is a size 12 English beading needle. These needles are 2 in. (5 cm) long, which is great to handle, and they are thin enough to fit through the tiniest of beads. It's a good idea to have a handful of needles in your tool kit, just in case a needle bends in half or breaks in the middle of a project.

Thread

I use nylon beading thread. Nylon thread comes in a variety of colors, so matching the thread color to the beads is easy. It's also widely available and relatively inexpensive.

Thread Conditioner

I always have thread conditioner handy. This helps stiffen the thread and prevents tangles. Another bonus for using thread conditioner is that the wax protects the thread from deterioration, so your stitched beads and hard work will last a very long time.

Bead Stopper

A Bead Stopper is a small clamp, which may be a spring coil or an electrical test clip. Bead Stoppers are wonderful for temporarily holding multiple beaded strands, clamping excessive thread while stitching, or holding anything temporarily hold before securing the thread or wire. You can never have enough Bead Stoppers! You may want to start off with six to eight stoppers in your inventory.

Beading Mat

A beading mat is a soft, felt-like fabric swatch (often made of Vellux) that is used as a place mat for making beadwork. Working on a beading mat will prevent your beads from scratching against a bare table and it will keep beads from escaping your workspace. I recommending having at least two or three in your tool kit so you have enough workspace to spread out all your beads and have fun.

Findings

Jewelry making components used to connect, bridge, and finish jewelry pieces are referred to as findings. Findings are available in a variety of metals, such as sterling silver, copper, gunmetal, brass, and pewter, and come in all sorts of decorative styles for you to choose from. When choosing a finding, keep in mind how it will look with your design and where it will be worn. A more fancy piece of jewelry may call for an extravagant clasp design.

Crimp Tubes

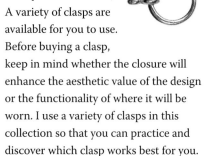

A crimp tube is a short soft metal cylinder used to secure beading wire. Crimp tubes come in various sizes and tube wall thickness. Usually, the precious metals, such as silver or gold-filled, have a thicker wall so crimping beading wire is easier and more secure and the crimp tube is less likely to break.

Clamshells

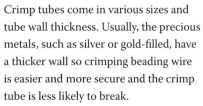

A clamshell (sometimes referred to as a bead tip) is a type of crimp cover that has two attached cups with a pin-sized hole between the area where the cups meet and also a hook attached to one of the cups. The purpose of this component is to pass the thread between the pin-sized hole between the cups and crimp it. Then the cups are squeezed together to conceal the crimp, and the clasp is attached to the hook. I recommend using clamshells only on lightweight jewelry, such as necklaces that use small beads or earrings. The clamshell can break if there is too much weight pulling on it and it's a real hassle to crimp it again.

Crimp Covers

A crimp cover is an opened round spacer bead that is later closed over an exposed crimp. The purpose of a crimp cover is to hide and protect the discomfort from the crimp tube. I love using these because they add that extra professional touch and attention to detail.

Head Pins

A head pin is a 1–3-in. (2–7 cm) piece of metal wire that has a flat, round pad at one end, similar to a sewing pin, but without the sharp point. Head pins are necessary for creating fringe by stringing on the beads and making a simple loop at the top before attaching it to the bead work. Be careful when shopping for head pins, because they come in various gauges. For these designs, I used 22-gauge head pins.

Eye Pins

Similar to a head pin, an eye pin has a pre-made simple loop instead of a flat pad. The simple loop at one end can speed up the process of making a chain or connecting beaded elements together. Like head pins, eye pins come in a variety of lengths and gauges, so note those attributes on the material lists when you go bead shopping.

Clasps

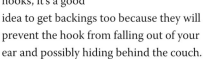

A variety of clasps are available for you to use. Before buying a clasp, keep in mind whether the closure will enhance the aesthetic value of the design or the functionality of where it will be worn. I use a variety of clasps in this collection so that you can practice and discover which clasp works best for you.

Earring Hooks

Earring hooks are used for making earrings. When purchasing earring hooks, it's a good idea to get backings too because they will prevent the hook from falling out of your ear and possibly hiding behind the couch.

Jump Rings

A jump ring is a single coil of wire used for connecting findings or beaded items together. Jump rings, like head pins, come in a variety of gauges and sizes. The sizes may change per project, but I recommend purchasing 22-gauge jump rings.

Jewelry Chain

Jewelry chain is a very delicate chain used for creating fringe or adding an extension to a jewelry piece. Jewelry chain is easy to find in most bead and craft stores and usually comes in a variety of metals for you to choose from. When you purchase chain, check to see if it is tarnished, damaged, or if the metal is chipping away. A quality chain has precise loops and no abrasion on the metal.

No. of Strands	
3	Very stiff beading wire that's great for holding a specific shape, but be careful when using it because it will kink or curl very easily (unless you desire it to do so).
7	Inexpensive beading wire that's not only great for beginner beaders wanting to experiment with stringing, but the combination of stiffness with flexibility makes this wire great for integrating it into bead weaving.
19	Generally considered a standard size, it's great for most stringing projects because of the strength of the wire and flexibility if offers.
21	Softer than 19 strand, this beading wire offers higher kink resistance and will create smooth shapes when woven with beads.
49	So far, the softest wire on the market and it's very flexible and highly kink-resistant. This wire is perfect for creating long pieces, such as lariats or matinee-style necklaces.

Diameter Guide	
.010	This wire is extremely thin, which is wonderful for stringing seed beads or gemstone beads with tiny holes.
.012	This wire size is slightly thicker than .010 and works great for stringing seed beads that are ready to be woven or stringing lightweight beads.
.014	This is the medium-size beading wire, and it's considered a standard size for most stringing projects. This wire is mostly used for the crystal weaving in this book because the wire is small enough to go through small-holed beads, yet it has structure and strength to keep its form.
.015	This wire is similar to .014; the only difference is that various companies manufacture different types of wire. The small size difference won't affect the look of your project.
.018	This wire size is considered heavy because of the thickness and sturdiness of the weight. This wire works great for stringing metal beads, stone beads, or large wood beads.
.019	This wire size is similar to .018.
.024	This is the thickest wire for bead stringing and is recommended for extremely large beads that are very heavy.

Beading Wire

Beading wire is a stainless steel cable wire coated with clear nylon plastic. The nylon coating protects the wire from tarnishing, breaking, and makes it comfortable to use. Beading wire comes in a variety of colors, gauges, and degrees of stiffness. The gauge of the wire is measured in diameter and as the diameter increases, so does the wire thickness.

Stiffness is measured by the number of strands twisted together before being coated with the nylon plastic. For instance, a 7 strand beading wire is stiffer than a 21 strand beading wire. The beading wire spool should be labeled with the diameter size and the number of strands within the wire. When purchasing wire, pay careful attention because these designs use a specific size for weaving the crystals.

The chart describes the variety of beading wires, number of strands, and sizes. When purchasing beading wire, choose an appropriate color and diameter as well.

Techniques

For a professional finish, practice the techniques in this section until you are comfortable with them. Here, you will learn how to start your project, add thread, and secure the thread, along with various other techniques needed to finish each project.

Starting a New Thread

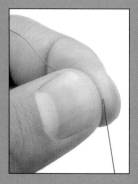

Attaching a New Thread

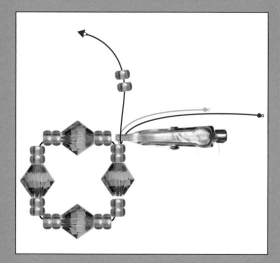

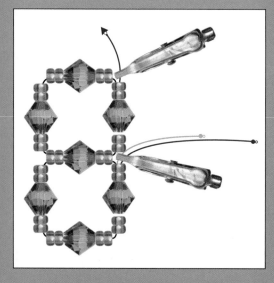

Starting a New Thread

Each project will start by creating the individual beaded components first. Cut an appropriate length of thread, thread your needle, and place a Bead Stopper on the thread. Working with a short piece of thread will prevent it from tangling and knotting up.

1 Cut a 36–45-in. (.9–1.4 m) length of thread.

2 Place the end of the thread between your thumb and index finger. (Press the thread into those fingers and place the needle over it with the hole of the needle flat to the fingers.) Push out the thread with your fingers to force the thread through the hole of the needle.

3 Place a Bead Stopper at the end of the thread, leaving a 5 in. (13 cm) tail, and you're ready to start your project.

Attaching New Thread

Sometimes you'll run out of thread mid-project. To add more thread and continue stitching a piece:

1 Stop stitching when the working thread is about 4 in. (10 cm) long.

2 Release the needle from that thread and re-thread the needle with new thread.

3 Place a Bead Stopper on the old thread and the new thread together at the base of the beadwork. The new thread must have a 4-in. tail in order to create a surgeon's knot (see note).

4 Continue stitching 5–7 beads with the new thread.

5 Stop stitching and place a Bead Stopper at the base of the beadwork on the new thread.

6 Remove the first Bead Stopper with the two threads and tie a surgeon's knot with those threads.

7 Remove the second Bead Stopper and continue stitching. Sew each thread separately into 1 in. (2.5 cm) of the beadwork and trim excess thread.

NOTE To tie a surgeon's knot: Tie one overhand knot by twisting two threads around each other once. Tie another one, except tie two twists and pull threads tight. To tie an overhand knot, take the cord and loop it over itself and pass the other cord inside of the loop and pull tight to create a knot.

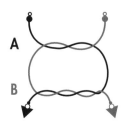

A

B

Securing Thread

A well-constructed jewelry piece hides all the thread. This process covers how to finish knotting the thread at the end of the beadwork stitching. Before finishing the last stitch of your beaded component, make sure to have at least 6–8 in. (15– 20 cm) of thread to tie an end knot.

1 Stitch into the bead next to the bead you came out of and leave a 3 in. (7.6 cm) loop. Use a Bead Stopper to clamp the base of the loop.

2 Stitch through the beads and exit through the bead where the loop begins.

3 Unclamp the loop and tie a surgeon's knot with the loop and thread.

4 Stitch loose threads 1 in. (2.5 cm) into the beadwork and trim excessive threads.

Crimping

Crimp a crimp bead to secure beading wire and attach clasps. Crimping is useful for all kinds of projects because of the versatility in crimping methods. A folded crimp is best for finishing a jewelry piece when attaching a clasp to the ends of the wire. A flattened crimp works well for tight spots that you can't reach with crimping pliers.

Folded Crimp

1 String a crimp bead and one half of the clasp on the beading wire.

2 Pass the beading wire back through the crimp. Only 1 in. (2.5 cm) of excess beading wire should be below the crimp.

3 Pull the wire and use your thumbnail to push the crimp closer to the clasp. The small wire loop should allow minimal movement of the clasp.

4 Place the crimp inside the second notch of the crimping pliers, separate the wires slightly and gently squeeze. Each wire should sit in one channel of the half-folded crimp.

5 Turn the crimp on its side and place it in the first notch of the crimping pliers. Squeeze the pliers firmly, and tug to make sure it will hold. The crimp will be cylindrical.

6 String a few beads over the excess wire to hide it.

7 To finish the other end, repeat steps 1–6, hiding the excess wire in 1 in. of the strung beads before tightening the loop. Crimp the tube, and then trim any excess wire with wire cutters.

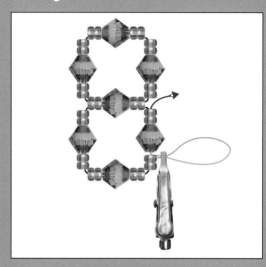

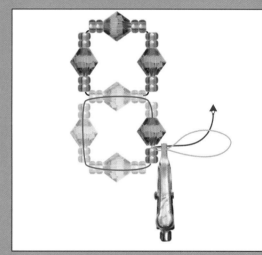

Folded Crimp

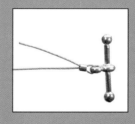

Flattened Crimp

Applying a Crimp Cover

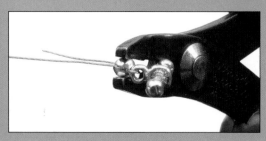

Attaching a Clamshell

Flattened Crimp

1 String a crimp on the beading wire.

2 Using chainnose pliers, gently squeeze the crimp tube in the mid section of the pliers.

3 Release the pliers and examine the crimp to see if it is flattened evenly. A flattened crimp looks like a flat square.

Applying a Crimp Cover

Crimp covers hide any exposed crimps and give your design a professional finish. To apply a crimp cover, follow the steps below.

1 Place the crimp cover in the first notch of the crimping pliers. The open part of the crimp cover should face the tip of the pliers.

2 Place the crimp cover over the folded crimp in a perpendicular position to the pliers.

3 Gently squeeze the pliers until the inside edges of the crimp cover are touching.

4 Release the pliers and use the first notch again to gently squeeze over the seam of the crimp cover bead.

Attaching a Clamshell

Clamshells are a great way to simplify crimping a wire and hiding the crimp. To attach a clamshell, follow the steps below.

1 Open the clamshell a little bit wider than it is already (this will make it easy to work inside of it) and pass the beaded wire up through the hole between the cups.

2 Pass the beading wire through a 1 mm crimp and allow the crimp to fall between the cups.

3 Squeeze the crimp with your bentnose pliers so it is flat, and trim the excess wire above it.

4 Squeeze the cups together and then place a clasp onto the hook and gently fold it in so that it is secure.

Making Simple Loops

Use simple loops to create fringe on beadwork or to bridge components together.

1 Measure ½ in. (1.3 cm) of wire from where the beads stop, and cut the end with a pair of double-flush cutters to create a blunt end on the wire.

2 Using roundnose pliers, grip the wire at the very tip.

3 Rotate the pliers counter clockwise, away from you, to wrap the wire around the pliers' jaws. Reposition the pliers as needed and continue wrapping to make a full circle. (You have formed a "P" shape.)

NOTE If there is too much wire between the bead and wire loop, cut as much wire off from the loop as there is space between the bead and where the loop starts and fold the loop again.

4 Grip the bottom part of the loop, where the loop begins, and rotate the pliers clockwise, towards you, until the loop is centered. In other words, break the neck of the loop so the head is straight. The loop will have a round head with a sharp bend in the neck.

5 To open a simple loop, use your bentnose pliers to grasp the open part of the loop and gently lift the wire up towards you. Place your component in the loop and close the loop by pressing the wire back down. If you bend the wire of the loop out, instead of toward you, the loop will lose its shape.

Opening and Closing Jump Rings

Jump rings are useful for bridging beaded components together.

1 Use chainnose pliers and bentnose pliers to grasp each side of the jump ring, with the opening at the top.

2 Gently push one of the pliers away from you and the other toward you. The open jump ring is now ready to use.

3 Close the jump ring by reversing steps 1 and 2. The seam of the jump ring should not have any space between it.

Making Jump Rings

In some instances, you may need to use an odd-sized jump ring. This technique guide will teach you how to make your own jump rings.

1 Cut 12 in (30 cm) of 22-gauge wire.

2 Coil the wire tightly around a pen (or dowel rod, depending on how big you want the inside diameter of the ring to be), and then carefully slip the wire coils off the pen.

3 Cut straight through the coils with your double-flush cutters, one at a time.

Making Simple Loops

Opening and Closing Jump Rings

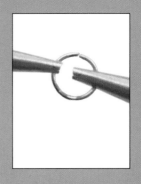 

Making Jump Rings

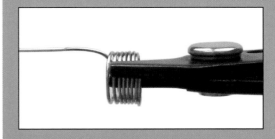

77

From the Designer

Writing a book was not something I planned or even expected to do. But it's amazing how everything progressed, and I'm glad things turned out the way it did. I started beading during my freshman year of high school. I took a class called Business Technology, and we were asked to develop and market an actual product. I happened to be the "CEO" of our fictitious company, and it was my teammate's idea to market jewelry to other high school students. I was sold on that idea, so after gathering the materials to make the jewelry, I decided to put together our products and have my teammates would take care of the paperwork. I really enjoyed making simple jewelry for my class project, and I decided to continue making it with the remaining supplies after the school year ended. The following summer, I remember watching a craft show that featured a brilliant artist, Lillian Todaro, who created wearable art, and I was completely inspired by it. I found various patterns online and put together my first collection of beadwork. Eventually, I began to learn the various stitches for bead weaving and learned how to compose my own designs.

I participated in various arts and craft shows, but found no satisfaction in selling my work. It wasn't until 2005 that I began to submit my work to various beading magazines, who then asked to publish my beading patterns. I also began to teach beading part time at various avenues, and I realized recently what I truly enjoyed about creating beaded jewelry: I love problem solving and creating something that is beautiful, very wearable, and easy for others to make themselves. Each piece I design is like solving a puzzle. Sometimes I see the finished design in my head, and then it suddenly shatters into a thousand pieces. I pick up those pieces and put them back together as I design. Often, many beaders run into problems and need a creative solution, which is what I try to solve with each design I create.

This book is my foray into authoring, and it was an amazing experience creating the designs and writing this book. I've met so many wonderful people and had the privilege to learn something new every step of the way.

Facebook:
www.facebook.com/nealay

Website:
www.behance.net/nealayjewelry